Old Nova Scotia Quilts

Scott Robson
Sharon MacDonald

Nimbus Publishing Limited

Nova Scotia Museum

© Crown copyright, Province of Nova Scotia, 1995
    99   5 4 3 2

Produced by the Nova Scotia Museum as part
of the Heritage and Culture Program of the
Department of Education and Culture,
Province of Nova Scotia

Minister: The Honourable John D. MacEachern
Deputy Minister: Robert P. Moody

Co-published by the Nova Scotia Museum and
Nimbus Publishing Limited

A product of the Nova Scotia Co-publishing Program

Design and typographic formatting: Arthur B. Carter, Halifax
Design consultant: Etta Moffatt
Imagesetting and film: Maritime Photoengravers, Halifax
Printing and binding: Printcrafters Inc., Winnipeg, MB

The research, exhibition, and publication of *Old Nova Scotian
Quilts* has been funded by the Museums Assistance Program,
Department of Canadian Heritage, and by the Nova Scotia
Museum.

Disponible en français sous le titre :
Courtepointes anciennes de la Nouvelle-Écosse.

Canadian Cataloguing in Publication Data

Robson, Scott. 1949-
Old Nova Scotian Quilts
Co-published by the Nova Scotia Museum.
ISBN 1-55109-118-6
1. Quilts—Nova Scotia. 2. Quilting—Nova Scotia—History. I.
MacDonald, Sharon, 1948- II. Nova Scotia Museum. III. Title.
TT835.R62 1995 746.46'09716   C95-950079-0

Front cover: Q 25
Back cover: Q 31
Title page: Q 33

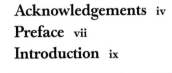

Contents

Acknowledgements

The exhibition at the Nova Scotia Museum, Halifax, 1993.

*T*his study of quilts in the province has benefitted from the contributions and encouragements of many individuals and the resources of many institutions.

First of all, without the Nova Scotia Museum's long-term commitment to building and maintaining historical collections, we would not have such an impressive group of quilts with which to work. It has taken many years to develop the collection to reflect some of the diversity of quiltmaking in the province.

Once the proposal for the research project and exhibition was developed, a major factor was the financial support of the Museums Assistance Program (MAP) of the federal Department of Canadian Heritage (formerly called the Department of Communications). MAP was the major source of funds for all three phases of the project (research and planning, production, and circulation), which included both the mounting of a nationally travelling exhibition and the realization of this book.

Co-workers at the Nova Scotia Museum have been supportive in many ways, offering suggestions for research or the exhibition plan; others contributed in less visible but important ways, through answering the telephone, taking care of the accounting, or dealing with office matters so that the work on quilts could continue. Dr Marie Elwood, recently retired as Chief Curator, History Section, Nova Scotia Museum, encouraged this project from the outset and made useful suggestions about research and planning. Besides the authors, the exhibition committee included Stephen Archibald and Joan Waldron. David Carter, John Kemp, Etta Moffatt, Dave Butler, and Kim Jarrett worked as designers and builders of the exhibition.

Sally Ross did more than translate all text for the exhibition and the book into French. In her attention to detail and her desire to give the most accurate and fluent French version, she often helped the writers to clarify the English. We were fortunate in our editor, Susan Lucy, Publications Section, Department of Supply & Services; she brought to her editorial tasks an additional enthusiasm for and knowledge of quilting. For the excellent photographs taken with the greatest care, thanks to Ron Merrick and Roger Lloyd, Media Services, Department of Education. Ken Burris, photographer for the Shelburne Museum, Vermont, proved to be most helpful in providing suggestions by phone.

A wide range of experts and museum curators took time to discuss quilts with the curator visiting from Nova Scotia. In England—Dorothy Osler, Newcastle-upon-Tyne; Rosemary E. Allan, The North of England

Open Air Museum, Beamish, County Durham; Judith Elsdon, The American Museum in Britain, Claverton Manor, Bath; and Shiela Betterton, recently retired from that institution. Also very helpful were visits to the National Art Library, the Crafts Council library, and the Victoria and Albert Museum, all in London. In Scotland–Naomi Tarrant, the Royal Museum of Scotland; Joyce Murray; and Janet K. Rae. In Northern Ireland–Valerie Wilson and Linda Ballard, Ulster Folk & Transport Museum, Cultra, County Down. In Wales–Christine Stevens, the Welsh Folk Museum, St. Fagan's, Cardiff; and Dr Ilid Anthony, formerly of that institution.

For research in the United States, thanks are extended to staff at the Museum of American Folk Art, New York: Gerard C. Wertkin, Director; Anne-Marie Reilly, registrar; and Stacy C. Hollander, curator of collections. This institution had the best collection of quilt books seen anywhere. As well, useful material was located at the New York Public Library; the Boston Public Library; and Old Sturbridge Village, Massachusetts. In Vermont, thanks to Celia Oliver, at the Shelburne Museum, custodian of one of the best-known collections of antique quilts in the United States.

Closer to home, many institutions, organizations and individuals have been generous with their time or have contributed valuable information. The largest single source for historical documents was the Public Archives of Nova Scotia (PANS). Staff members were always helpful, but special thanks are due to Margaret Campbell and Gail Judge. Kate Currie's expert knowledge of the collection at the Beaton Institute, University College of Cape Breton, enabled the researcher to make the most of limited time in Cape Breton. Various archives for the United Church (including old Methodist and Presbyterian records), Baptist Church, and Anglican Church proved to be mines of information on quilting activity in women's church and missionary societies. Very special thanks to Carolyn Earle of the Maritime Conference Archives (United Church) and Pat Townsend of the Acadia University Archives, where the Baptist records are held.

Teresa Osborne and Sandy Savage, Women's Institutes of Nova Scotia headquarters, Truro, allowed access to all their old records as did staff of the Nova Scotia Division of the Canadian Red Cross. Rocky Jones, who initiated an oral history project in the Black communities of Nova Scotia in the 1970s, allowed access to the unpublished transcripts of the Black Historical and Educational Research Organization (HERO). Thanks to Sheila Stevenson and Deborah Trask of the Nova Scotia Museum for suggesting examination of two other oral history projects undertaken by the Nova Scotia Museum in the communities of New Ross and Jeddore.

Helen Pugh of the British Red Cross Archives in Surrey, England, was exceptional in her assistance and support of research in Britain (carried out by mail); and B.P. Burgers of Het Nederlandse Rode Kruis (Netherlands Red Cross) was also helpful. Nan Harvey, archivist of the Colchester Historical Society, Truro, and Win Harvey, a volunteer who took time to show relevant artifacts from that collection, were very co-operative. Further thanks to Janet Maltby, Cape Breton Centre for Heritage and Science; Eric Ruff and Laura Bradley of the Yarmouth County Museum; Ralph Getson

Eaton's catalogue for fall & winter 1923-24

and Jim Tupper, Fisheries Museum of the Atlantic; Elizabeth Crouse, Nova Scotia 4-H Council; Peter Sanger, Nova Scotia Agricultural College Archives; Donna Smith, Parkdale-Maplewood Museum; Shirley Penney, Breton Quilters; Karen Anderson, *Chatelaine* magazine; Sandra Thomas, New Brunswick Women's Institute; Lena Klassen, Stearns Canada; Carol Ricketts, McClelland & Stewart, Inc.; Dianne Huck, *Patchwork & Quilting* magazine; Gillian Webster, Cultural Affairs Library; the Admiral Digby Historical Society; staff at Fortress Louisbourg, Parks Canada; Halifax City Regional Library; and the Canadian Museum of Civilization.

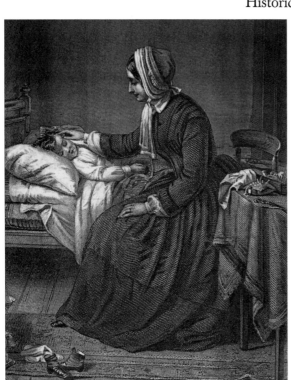

"The Mother's Blessing" (detail), Godey's Lady's Book*, Philadelphia, March 1858. A sewing project lies on the table, ready to be worked on in spare moments.*

Alexander Leighton was ever patient and generous, giving permission to use wonderful photographs of quilting taken in the 1950s for the Stirling County Study. Mary Nickerson, in response to a newsletter query, began gathering information and photos on quilts in her area of the province; her discoveries proved most useful. Other individuals have also contributed pieces of information to the story: Iona Baxter, Phyllis Blades, Audrey Densmore, Alphonse Deveau, Norman Duncan, Evelyn Edwards, Douglas Eagles, Margie Glabay, Rosamund Hope, Jean Jess, Doreen Langille, Kay Matheson, Muriel MacAloney, Lorna MacLean, Judith Mader, Jessie McCully, Marial Mosher, Vernon Spurr, Ruth Symes, Lloyd Wentzel, Marion Wentzell, and Helen Dacey Wilson. Grateful appreciation is extended to all the correspondents in Great Britain who took time to write and send photos of the Canadian Red Cross quilts that they received during the war.

Quilters have, of course, been instrumental in this study. Not always known by name, they have contributed information or have offered useful comments over many years as quilts from the museum collection were shown in slide lectures around the province or displayed in exhibitions. Two quilters have been of special importance: Polly Greene and Barbara (Paterson) Robson.

There are always countless influences in the creation of a book. All the previously published writers on the history of quilting in Canada, the United States, and Britain have contributed greatly. Without their work, it would have been impossible to see and study so many quilts. The list of Selected Books and Articles acknowledges these people by name.

Finally, the original record keepers—diarists, journalists, or minute keepers, as well as the writers of local histories—have contributed the primary and secondary sources for the Nova Scotian story. Because extensive use of footnotes would have made the text very cluttered, these have been kept to a minimum. For a complete list of sources in which quilt information was found, see the reference section at the end of the book.

Preface

Detail of Q 25

*T*he Nova Scotia Museum has a wonderful collection of quilts. With Nova Scotia's rich heritage of quiltmaking, it is fitting that the provincial museum should take a special interest in preserving examples of this tradition, and in presenting them in this book and in the exhibition, *Old Nova Scotian Quilts.*

Although the Provincial Museum was established in 1868 and its collection dates back to 1831, almost all of the material dealing with the cultural history of the province has been gathered since 1900. The museum acquired its first quilt in 1958, and only a few others before the late 1960s. As with other artifacts at that time, many textiles were collected for use as household furnishings in museum restorations. By the 1970s, staff were making a more concerted effort to develop the textile collection to represent various styles and construction techniques. The museum now owns over 175 quilts; 100 of those are carefully held in the provincial reserve collection. Among them are the two oldest quilts known in the province (c1810), the finest old appliqué quilt, an extraordinary white quilt with matching valance, and a very handsome crazy quilt with lace edge. Only a few of these quilts have been exhibited or published.[1] For the first time, more than fifty quilts from the collection are widely available to study and enjoy.

Most of the quilts illustrated here belong to the Nova Scotia Museum and were made in the province. Following from the exhibition, this book contains two levels of information on quilts: visual and documentary. The quilts are arranged visually according to type of construction of the quilt tops—pieced, log cabin, crazy (and other silk quilts), wholecloth (including white), and appliqué. The pieced quilt section is by far the largest, reflecting the dominance of this type among old quilts in the province. The documentary material explores the social history of quiltmaking in the province, based on details found in diaries, newspapers, and inventories, as well as records of the Red Cross, and church and women's groups.

Some of this information is about specific quilts, while other details add to our understanding of the lives of Nova Scotians who made and used quilts. Just as a quilt is composed of hundreds of scraps of fabrics, selected, cut into shape, and assembled, the record of quilting in the province is composed of a diverse collection of fragments, pieced together to form a large and impressive story.

While a considerable body of research on quiltmaking has originated in the United States, the interest in quilt history has become international in scope. With this publication, the story of quiltmaking in Nova Scotia unfolds. It is hoped that this work will serve as a spur to further research and discovery.

This map indicates where each quilt originated (numbers refer to the quilts in Chapter 5). That there are more locations marked in one county than in another does not necessarily mean that quilting was more common there; we selected quilts to represent types rather than communities. Development of a public collection depends on gifts from individuals and on purchases from dealers, sales, or auctions. The heavily marked sections of the map reflect where there is more active trade in antiques. There is also variation related to cultural origin; for example, in areas with a stronger concentration of Scottish settlement, weaving was more widespread and many people used blankets rather than quilts.

Local people often prefer to have their family treasures kept near where they were made and used. For those who are interested in seeing more quilts from a particular area of the province, enquiries should be made at community museums.

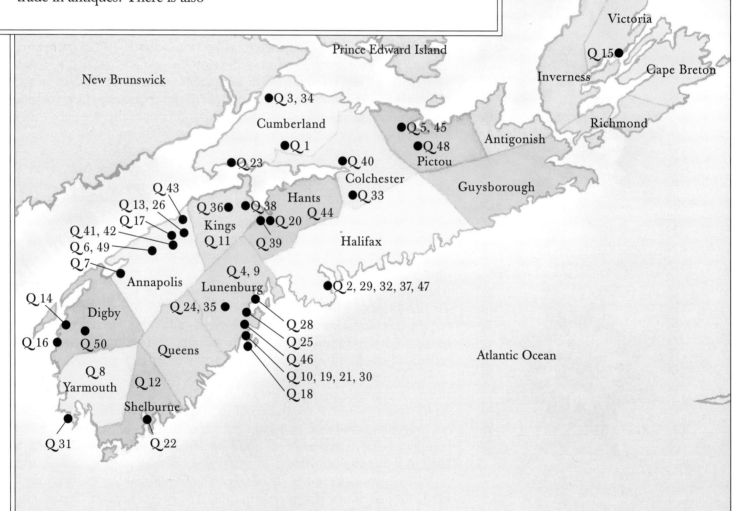

Introduction

Things that are always with us and always dependable have a quality of invisibility. From cradle to grave we are surrounded by textiles, yet how many of us ever stop to consider that a complete miracle has been performed by the making of a piece of cloth. The usefulness of textiles is undisputed; life would be unthinkable without them and they can also be beautiful, with a subtle beauty that is satisfying to the senses of both sight and touch.

Dorothy K. Burnham, *The Comfortable Arts: Traditional Spinning and Weaving in Canada*[1]

*Q*uilts. The very word calls up warm thoughts—of mothers and grandmothers, of love, comfort, and security, of learning to sew, favourite patterns, bright colours, and recollections of thrift during harder times.

Because quilts dwell in the most intimate of our interior spaces—the bedroom—and because they hold meaning on several levels, they are rather unique in the world of artifacts. They are associated with very personal moments of joy and sorrow, with birth and death. In the past, quilts provided essential physical warmth, but they also gave emotional comfort as familiar, cozy articles of bedding. And so often they were made by a loved one. Sometimes in stark surroundings, quilts provided a splash of colour and design, enlivening a space that might otherwise have been cheerless. Quilts made with scraps of fabric from well-loved, worn clothing also contain family history. Many memories are wrapped up in such quilts.

In addition to these personal associations, quilts have been part of a broader social history. Women[2] came together (and continue to do so) to help one another complete quilts for their families, for neighbours and strangers in need, and to raise money to support community work. For many, quilting has always been a part of daily life. Early lessons were learned at the elbows of older women at home, when visiting neighbours, or at the church hall. This largely rural tradition was conveyed from one generation to another, into the mid-1900s.

There has been much interest and revived activity in quilting in the last twenty years. This can be traced, in large part, to a major exhibition[3] in 1972 of American quilts, assembled by Jonathan Holstein and Gail van der Hoof. Few people now affected by the 'quilting bug' saw that exhibition or book,[4] but the ripple effects touched many. Quilts gained stature as fine examples of traditional craft; they were given more serious consideration on the basis of artistic expression and were exhibited more frequently in major galleries and museums. Furthermore, the field of women's studies has enriched the study of quilts and of the context in which they were made.

There had been another revival half a century before. The very first book on old quilts, *Quilts: Their Story and How to Make Them*, by Marie

Webster, was published in 1915. More quilt books appeared in the late 1920s and early 1930s, such as Ruth E. Finley's *Old Patchwork Quilts and the Women Who Made Them* (1929) and Carrie Hall and Rose G. Kretsinger's *The Romance of the Patchwork Quilt in America* (1935). As a sign of a growing interest in antiquarian artifacts in the United States, the first issue of *Antiques* magazine appeared in January 1922; an item on a patchwork quilt was included in the February issue.

In Nova Scotia, these revivals simply enhanced a continuous and active tradition. Quilts remained essential in many rural households, and making them continued to be a meaningful social activity, even as the quilting revival of the 1970s began.

This book showcases the best of the Nova Scotia Museum collection. The majority of these quilts were made during the mid- to late-1800s; the most recent quilt was made in 1952. Although this is not a 'how-to' book, many readers may find designs that they will want to use. In the Gallery of Quilts (Chapter 5), the inclusion of measurements and other relevant details on the geometry and design elements should assist them in drafting patterns.

As well, this is an exploration of how our quiltmaking tradition developed and what it shares with the traditions of other places. Through studying the quilts in the museum's collection as well as researching the historical, geographical, and social factors that have contributed to maintaining this long and dynamic tradition, a broad picture emerges. Quilters and non-quilters alike will find much to interest them in the Nova Scotian quilt story.

CHAPTER 1

The Cultural Fabric of Nova Scotia

*N*ova Scotia lies at the very edge of the North American continent, nearly an island but for the Isthmus of Chignecto connecting the province to New Brunswick and the rest of Canada. It juts out into the North Atlantic, perched part way between Great Britain and the United States. In the 1700s and 1800s, at a time when most of inland Canada was still 'in the backwoods', Nova Scotia had frequent contact by sea with the American seaboard and with Britain. So too is our quilting tradition part way between those two places, like many of our customs and even our way of speaking. The notion of accent may express something of the identity of quiltmaking in Nova Scotia.

The oldest surviving examples of quilts in the province date from about 1810. By that time, the population had become predominantly British. The previous century was filled with conflict between two major European powers with interests in the area: the French and the English. However, they were not the only groups here.

"View from Fort Needham near Halifax" (detail), by G.I. Parkyns, 1801. NSM 76.20.3

The first inhabitants of Nova Scotia were the Mi'kmaq, an Algonkian-speaking people living in the region today known as the Atlantic provinces, as well as parts of Québec and Maine. Norse explorers and Basque fishermen visited these shores but did not stay. The first permanent European settlement in North America north of the Gulf of Mexico, the Habitation at Port-Royal, was built by the French in 1605.

In the 1600s, the region known as Acadia (Nova Scotia and New Brunswick today) became a battleground for continental conflict. In 1710, the British drove the French from Port-Royal and renamed it Annapolis Royal and by 1713 all of mainland Nova Scotia passed into British hands. At Louisbourg on Cape Breton Island, the French began to build a fortress, but that too eventually fell to the British in 1745, only to be returned by treaty. Then in 1749 the British built their new seaport capital at Halifax as a strategic post against Louisbourg and Québec. Britain wanted to establish more colonies in North America, extending their influence all the way up the eastern seaboard from Virginia. Finally in 1758, Louisbourg was taken again, and Nova Scotia remained a British colony thereafter.

During this turbulent period, the Acadians, who lived peacefully in scattered small settlements, were expelled from their lands in 1755 and were deported further south to the American colonies. Many later returned, but their homes had been destroyed and their farms taken over in the 1760s by American settlers known as Planters.

In the 1750s, the British encouraged German and Swiss people to immigrate to the colony, settling at Halifax and Lunenburg. Then the Scots arrived, first at Pictou in 1773 and later in Cape Breton. After the American Revolution, loyalists immigrated in the 1780s to take up land grants; in this group there was a substantial number of Black settlers. In the early 1800s, the English, Scottish, and American influx continued with the addition of settlers from Ireland after the Napoleonic Wars.

"Grand Pré, and Basin of Minas, from Wolfville", by F.B. Schell, 1884. NSM 78.99

We have not been able to identify distinct quiltmaking traditions among the Acadians, Blacks, Germans, or other groups that settled in the province, or among the Mi'kmaq. Women from various cultural origins made quilts during the late 1800s and early 1900s. However, it appears that they learned the basic techniques from the British tradition, perhaps introducing cultural preferences for colour or pattern.

Quilts that survive in North America from the 1700s resemble quilts made in Britain.[1] The range of patterns was limited at that time, with motifs commonly set in pieced bands that framing a central panel or square.

Favourite motifs were composed of squares and triangles ('windmill', 'broken dishes', 'flying geese'). Gradually in the early 1800s, Americans changed and extended that tradition considerably, and their quilts developed a distinctive appearance, particularly through the use of pattern block construction. With continuing influx of settlers from the eastern United States, block construction also became common in Nova Scotian quilts.[2]

By the late 1800s in Britain, factory-made goods had become widely available and functional quiltmaking diminished. However, well after 1900, people in rural areas of Canada and the United States remained dependent on traditional crafts such as quilting because of practical need. In fact, the quilting tradition flourished in places like Nova Scotia.

People often ask whether Nova Scotian quilts differ from those of Britain or the United States. They share many similar characteristics. Differences are more difficult to identify because they are subtle. Just as a common language is spoken with regional variations, so too there are regional accents in quilts. Our accent may be more apparent to others. A provincial quilt registry would yield a much larger sampling for further study, and with that data, we may be able to discern a distinctive Nova Scotian accent, as well as some variation within regions of the province.

"Lochaber Lake..." near Antigonish, by W.S. Moorsom, in Letters from Nova Scotia, *London, 1830*

"Province House, Holles Street, Halifax", by W.S. Moorsom, 1830

CHAPTER 2

The Written History of Quilts
in Nova Scotia

*A*lthough the French were the first Europeans to set up permanent settlement in Nova Scotia, there are almost no documentary sources recording details about the daily life of the Acadians who lived here. At Louisbourg,[1] estate inventories from the early 1700s describe some articles of bedding, most of which would have been brought from France. Otherwise, the earliest references to quilts found in Nova Scotia are in English and date from the mid-1700s.

Halifax Gazette, *24 August 1754;*
Massachusetts Historical Society

Inventories and Newspapers

A complete survey of inventories would take more time than was available for this project, but a cursory look reveals a number of interesting findings. Our oldest references to quilts, patchwork, and quilted petticoats support research in the United States and Britain. Contrary to popular belief, quilts were not 'make-do' items pieced together from old scraps, but were bedcoverings that only the well-to-do could afford.

As might be expected, inventories for the estates of wealthy people are the most detailed; except on rare occasion, these were registered in the names of men rather than women. The level of description depended entirely on the inventory taker, and we can be grateful that some thought it worthwhile to note colour, fabric, or construction in their lists.

The earliest dated reference occurs in the *Halifax Gazette* of 24 August 1754, where notice is made of a quilt "to be sold at private sale by William Craft Auctioneer, at the Auction Room behind Capt. Cooke's near the beech". When Elinor Fallon died in 1771, she left behind "one Quilt *her own making*" (our emphasis). No other inventory made such an observation. The 1772 inventory of Martha Harrington of Newport, Hants County, lists one quilted petticoat. However, the 1782 inventory of shopkeeper Philip Knaut of Lunenburg is much more descriptive, listing eleven black, four pink, and seven sky blue "Quilted Petty coats... In the Store below stairs"; the large number may indicate that they were imported, probably from Britain.

Quilted petticoat, probably made in England, late 1700s. NSM 49.8.12. Worn by a woman in the Uniacke family, the faded silk satin was originally canary yellow.

By 1785, advertisers in newspapers were offering "patches" along with "callico stripes", "quiltings", and other related materials. In 1790, the *Halifax Journal* advertised "Patches, India, $2 each". Although that price was probably for a packet of patches, it nevertheless indicates that a person had to have money to purchase such choice items. The same year, "Patches, Chintz" were offered for sale in the *Royal Gazette & Nova Scotia Advertiser*. In the 1797 inventory of Elizabeth Earle, "some patchwork" is listed as worth £ 0/2/3.[2]

The following notice from *The Nova Scotia Royal Gazette*, a Halifax newspaper, gives yet another indication of the value placed on patchwork.

December 2, 1802

Whereas a most daring ROBBERY was committed at the house of Benjamin James, near the upper Blockhouse, on Saturday between the hours of 10 and 11 o'clock in the forenoon, by a person in a sailor's long jacket, dark pantaloons, and a red handkerchief round his neck, who opened the fore door, and the door of the parlor, in which stood a cott, and from which he took and carried off, one pair of blankets, and a handsome patch-worked counterpane; whoever will discover the offender so that he may be brought to justice, shall receive a handsome reward, from

BENJAMIN JAMES

Diaries

After inventories and newspapers, women's diaries offer some of the earliest references to quilting.

An important document in American quilt history is the diary of Anna Green Winslow, a schoolgirl in Boston in the 1770s. Born in Cumberland, Nova Scotia, she was the daughter of Anna Green and Joshua Winslow, who were originally from Boston but had settled in Nova Scotia. At age ten, Anna was sent to live with an aunt in Boston in order to obtain proper schooling, which was not available in rural Cumberland at the time. Her journal was encouraged by her parents as a way of improving her writing skills as well as keeping them informed of her activities.[3] It is a lively account of the life of a privileged young girl of the period, and demonstrates the emphasis placed on handwork training for girls. Apparently she tired of one sewing project because Anna mentions on 18 April 1772 that she has exchanged the piece of patchwork on which she had been working for "a pair of curious lace mitts with blue flaps", her hopes frustrated that the patchwork could ever grow "large enough to have cover'd a bed". One can well imagine that the patience required for such a project was not the strong suit of an imaginative twelve-year-old who had so many other activities vying for her attention. In spite of Anna's failure to complete her project, she left behind the record of it—to date, the earliest Nova Scotia-related reference to patchwork.

Anna Green Winslow; from the 1894 edition of her diary

Mary Ann Norris; PANS

The first quilting references found in diaries written in Nova Scotia are those of Mary Ann Norris who lived at Starr's Point, Kings County, Almira Bell of Shelburne, and Margaret Dickie Michener of Hantsport. These diaries were were written between 1820 and 1850. While not wealthy, these women were better educated than many of their contemporaries. From these diaries, the social significance of quilting is evident. By contrast, the diarists who wrote about quilting in the late 1800s and early 1900s tended to be less descriptive of social times and recorded quilting as one of the many household tasks. These later diarists were generally farm women with little leisure time; they recorded daily life in a terse, less descriptive style than did the earlier writers. This suggests that for more privileged women in the later period, quilting was not so important in their social life, perhaps because there were more options open to them.

The following excerpts about quilting reveal something of the social world of Mary Ann Norris (1800-1880). She was the daughter of a minister and through her mother was connected to several influential families in Nova Scotia. These entries were written when she was in her early twenties.

"The Quilting Party", Godey's Lady's Book, *Philadelphia, September 1849, illustrating an article by T.S. Arthur that describes the 1820s. Parks Canada, Ottawa*

Sept. 24th, 1823
Catherine and I went to help Mrs Allison quilt. Spent a very pleasant afternoon.

Oct. 18th, 1823
Margaret Allison, Elizabeth and Lavinia Whidden came to help us quilt. John Allison came in after tea for a short time.

March 23, 1825
Miss Bayard, Sarah Campbell, Mary and Margaret Allison, Lavinia Whidden, Robert Buskirk and Elisha DeWolf dined with us. The ladies came to help us quilt but the gentlemen were so troublesome all the morning that they would not allow them to do much.

March 30th, 1825
Catherine [and I] went to assist Mrs Harry Borden patch up a quilt and met quite a pleasant party there and had a much more agreeable evening than I had anticipated. She entertained us very well....

The carefree social life of her youth changed when Mary Ann's mother died, and she took on the responsibility of caring for her rather difficult and sickly father. After the Reverend Mr Norris died in 1834, Mary Ann continued to run the household and farm with some hired help.

Another writer of the period was Almira Bell of Shelburne, a school teacher in Barrington for a number of years. Although her home town was not exactly a teeming metropolis or world fashion centre, she seemed to think Barrington was quite an outpost when she first arrived.

Sunday 20th [July 20, 1834]—I went to the Head with the rest of the Island girls - the Chapel was crowded, and the heat excessive - I could not help contrasting the present appearance of the ladies, in respect of costume, to what it was when I first came to Barrington - plain calico <u>then</u>, and <u>now</u> nothing but Gras de Naples and leghorn bonnets - my thoughts ought to have been better employed for Mr P. preached a very good sermon.

Nevertheless, she fit in well with the local young people, and along with other social events she recorded that on Wednesday, 24 September 1834, "Hannah C. had a quilting today." A couple of weeks later she wrote that "Hannah Crowell had a quilting party to which I was invited and went—in the evening Lovitt Wilson, James Doane and Corning C[–] came and we had quite a singing meeting."

Margaret Dickie Michener operated a school, taught music, and had a lending library at her father's house in Hantsport in the 1840s. After her first husband died in 1850, she did further studies at Horton Academy before returning to teaching. Eventually she remarried and moved to the United States with her new husband, Robert McCullogh. The diaries were presented in regular installments through the mid-to-late-1920s in *The Acadian*, a Wolfville (Kings County) newspaper. Rich in personal and social detail, the diaries are a marvelous record of life in small-town Nova Scotia in the mid-1800s. Of numerous references to quilting, the following excerpts clearly emphasize quilting as an important social function:

Aug. 7th, 1849—Friday afternoon Ruth Holmes, Abigail, Harriet Holmes and I were at Mrs Enoch Marsters to a quilting.

March 5th, 1850— Ann had a quilting today and in the evening Simeon and I went up there.

Aug. 20th, 1850—I had an invitation today to a quilting at Mercy's.

Nov. 2nd, 1851—Mr D. Huntly called to invite the young folks to a quilting next day to meet his bride, that he has lately brought here.

It is interesting to note that nowhere in the historical records in Nova Scotia has the word 'bee' turned up in reference to quilting. In the Michener diary, mention is made of a sewing bee, but never a quilting bee. In Nova Scotia today, although that term is sometimes used by modern quilters and by people who are writing about the 'olden days', traditional

Inventory of some or that part of the movable Estate of the late Mr David Eaton of Cornwallis deceased which is to be divided among the seven brethren, taken the 21st of July A.D. 1803

	£	s	d
7 Blankets 74/ 1 piecework Bed quilt 25/	*4*	*19*	*0*
1 Green Bed quilt	*1*	*2*	*6*
1 Blue Bed quilt 7/6 1 Coverlid 7/6		*15*	*0*
1 Shaloon Bed quilt 22/6 1 Coverlid 4/	*1*	*6*	*6*
1 Old Bed quilt 4/ 1 Coverlid 4/		*10*	
4 Underbeds 15/ 1 pair of shoes 4/		*19*	

Patchwork and piecework may well have been interchangeable terms.

quilters still refer to a 'quilting' or a 'quilting party'. The term 'frolic' was also used, sometimes in connection with quilting and sometimes with haying or other activities where neighbours came together to help each other.

Q. What did older people do for fun?

A. They got together and made quilts and made pillow cases and they made their curtains and they had what we call a frolic and they would go to one person's house... and all chip in and make a quilt... we would go all through the neighbourhood all the time making these quilts. And the younger children would go coasting....

> Informant from Bridgetown, Annapolis County; HERO Oral History Project[4]

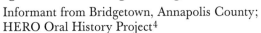

A member of the Baptist Church sewing circle gets help making a quilt in the 'double wedding ring' pattern for her daughter who will be married soon. Freeport, Digby County, 1951. Photo by John Collier, Jr.; Stirling County Study

Quilting party at St. Croix, Hants County, 1948. Helen Creighton collection; PANS

Piecing together quilts was the work carried on during the afternoon while sitting on Mrs Guild's spacious verandah.

> Middleton Church Sewing Circle minute book, Middle Musquodoboit, Halifax County, 25 August 1926

Changing Social Patterns

In the late 1700s and early 1800s, quilts were to be found in wealthier households, and quilting parties were a form of social life among the more affluent. As the nineteenth century progressed, a shift in social patterns occurred, driven by a number of factors.

As educational opportunities opened for upper and middle class women, they began to devote more of their time to pursuing activities that took them out of the private sphere and into the public. Only a few women entered professions, but many more devoted themselves to religious and charitable work. As they witnessed the plight of the poor and disenfranchised, they recognized the limitations that they themselves experienced because of their sex. Women, who at one time might have come together for quilting parties, were now busy addressing social issues. Some engaged in educational and cultural pursuits. Although many women still took pride in producing a fine quilt for use in the bedroom, by the turn of the century,

fewer women of privilege spent their time in such production. During the late Victorian period, these women were more interested in making silk and crazy quilts to display in the parlour.

On the other hand, women of lesser means were able to take advantage of technological changes occurring in the textile industry, and, with mass production of cheaper, affordable fabrics, women were able to put their resourcefulness to advantage in the creation of quilts.

In Nova Scotia, with its largely rural-based economy centred around a mixture of farming, fishing, and lumbering, quilting continued to be a vital social activity. Many men in this maritime province were engaged in sea-faring work. Women managed households, often maintaining farms and having to go for long stretches with little money. They had strong informal support networks among female relatives and friends. Making quilts was still necessary to keep the family supplied with bedding, and it was significant as a community occasion, where women could combine their socializing with productive and sometimes charitable activity.

[We continued] sewing on the quilt, while animated discussion was engaged in, on Political, Social and Personal Combinations.

Woman's Auxiliary minute book, St. Andrew's Anglican Church, Mulgrave, Guysborough County, 8 January 1924

Handing Down the Tradition–Children Sewing

Traditions are not maintained if children do not learn them. A major change in our present world from that of the past is in the training of children and, more specifically, in the education of girls. It is now possible for a girl to enter adulthood without having learned to thread a needle.

In the past, sewing and patchwork were considered an essential part of a girl's education, and although the era and the social class in which she lived might determine the kind of sewing projects taken on, almost all girls had some training. The eighteenth-century diarist Anna Green Winslow learned plain and fancy sewing. As discussed in *No Place Like Home*, a girl in Anna's social class was expected to be practical but also capable of ornamental refinements.[5]

Educational opportunities were limited for the majority of girls, but the schooling Anna received in Boston was typical for the period and her class. Although academic courses were taught, needlework, drawing, music, and foreign languages such as French and Italian were considered more important in the 'finishing' of a girl, preparing her to take on her future role as mother, housewife, and gracious host.

Learning to sew, however, was not restricted to those who could afford to attend private schools. When childhood activities were not so clearly delineated from those of adulthood, girls learned domestic skills from their mothers and grandmothers, gradually taking on more challenging tasks and responsibilities as they matured.

Period references to children quilting indicate that sewing was an integral and formative part of growing up in the nineteenth and early-to-mid-twentieth centuries. As well, during the nineteenth century, religious training held great significance. A young girl would follow her mother's example in spiritual matters. By the 1850s, the missionary movement in North America was strong, with a number of influential missionaries from

Then hearing from one of our missionaries in Suryana[?] of the suffering caused in the Girls' School by the cold weather, on account of the scarcity of bedclothes, we went to work, made a box of quilts and comfortables. As the small children could not help in the quilting, though they pieced one of the quilts, we gave them little cotton work bags to make and fill with anything they liked for the children in the kinder-garten department.

Annual Report, Tabernacle Mission Band,
Yarmouth, January 1894

Alice Wetmore (right) with her family on board ship; Yarmouth County Historical Society

Nova Scotia travelling to foreign lands to spread the Christian gospel. Women's missionary societies were formed, followed by junior groups and mission bands for children. For women and girls, Christian duty often included sewing and quilting for the missions.

In July 1852, an article appeared in the *Missionary Register*, a Presbyterian newspaper, describing the recent formation of the Juvenile Society of the Missionary Society in Dayspring, Lunenburg County. Thirty girls, aged nine to thirteen years, were busy raising money for supplies to send to girls' schools in missionary stations. Among the list of articles being sent were "patchwork, needles, thread, scissors, thimbles".

The Rev. John and Charlotte Geddie were Presbyterian missionaries from Pictou, Nova Scotia, who went to the New Hebrides in the South Pacific where they carried out evangelical work for many years. Both of them wrote letters back to Nova Scotia, which were regularly published in the *Missionary Register*. In a letter dated November 1853, Mrs Geddie wrote a post-script: "Patchwork, or rather pieces to make patchwork, are very useful to teach little girls to sew." As part of the Christianizing process, the island children were taught domestic skills and instilled with Western values.

Girls continued to sew for missions abroad and for local charities up until the mid-1900s, not only within church groups but also through other organizations, such as 4-H Club and Junior Red Cross. Although youth groups undoubtedly played a large part in encouraging girls to sew and quilt, most girls began their training at home with women in the family. That there was less distinction made between work and play can be seen in the following diary excerpts.

October 17, 1902
Mother is making a quilt of flowered cretonne with a layer of sheep's wool between. The wool has to be carded with wire carders, put between two sheets of cretonne and knotted with yarn. We have been doing the knotting which is easy.

March 4, 1903
After ten weeks holidays, we were back at school lessons today. Mother made another quilt which we helped to knot....

The writer was Alice Wetmore, the adolescent daughter of a sea captain from Yarmouth. She wrote a lively account of a voyage with her mother and younger sister, as the *Mary A. Law* plied its trade in the West Indies and South America. Living at sea may have been an unusual experience for a young girl, but Alice's participation in making a quilt was typical for girls from many backgrounds in Nova Scotia.

According to the HERO oral history project, quilting was very much a part of girlhood in the rural Black communities of the province. When asked what she did for entertainment when she was little, one woman (born in 1887) replied, "We made quilts, we made mats, and we made stockings and we made bags." Another (born in 1893) answered, "For one thing I tried to play music, sewing, making quilts, mats... and cooking."

Perhaps part of the reason quiltmaking remained a strong tradition in rural Nova Scotia was because, in a world of limited resources, the opportunity and challenge of creating something of beauty, even with odd scraps of fabric, was satisfying. With quilting, not only was it possible for women and children to combine artistic expression with the making of essential bedding, but they could have a good social time as well.

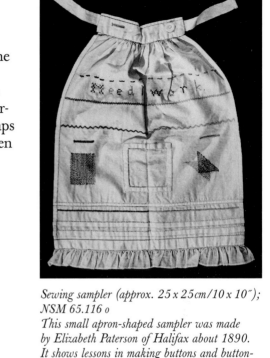

Sewing sampler (approx. 25 x 25 cm/10 x 10˝);
NSM 65.116 o
This small apron-shaped sampler was made by Elizabeth Paterson of Halifax about 1890. It shows lessons in making buttons and buttonholes, hemming, gathering, tucking, mending, patching, making a ruffle, and embroidery.

What little girl does not recollect her first pieces of patchwork, the anxiety for fear the pieces would not fit, the eager care with which each stitch was taken, and the delight in finding the bright squares successfully blended into the pretty pattern. Another square and another, and the work begins to look as if in time it might become a quilt.

Godey's Lady's Book,
Philadelphia, February 1857

Girls ironing doll clothing, about 1880, U.S.A.
Half of a stereo photo; NSM 92.33.64

21

Women's Institute

It would be impossible to write about quilts and quiltmaking in Nova Scotia in the twentieth century without discussing the Women's Institute. No other single organization had such an impact in keeping alive the traditional craft of quiltmaking. However, the Women's Institute would not have been able to maintain and continue the tradition had quilting not been an on-going, vital part of rural women's lives.

Although there are now Women's Institutes and affiliated groups throughout the world (under the name of Associated Country Women of the World), the very first Women's Institute was founded in Stoney Creek,

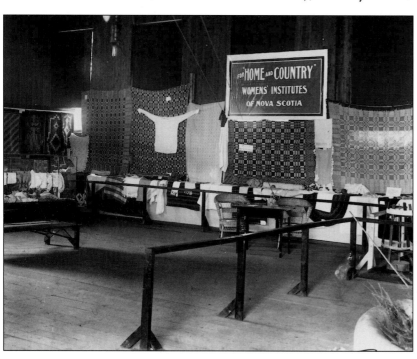

Women's Institute exhibit of weaving, knitting, sewing, mat hooking and quilting; Nova Scotia Provincial Exhibition, Halifax, 1915. Photo by Gauvin & Gentzel; NSM 38.176

Ontario, by a young farm woman, Adelaide Hoodless. When Hoodless lost her first-born child to illness at eighteen months, the doctor told her that the death could have been prevented with the use of pasteurized milk. Hoodless decided that in order to spare others from experiencing a similar tragedy, the education of rural women needed to be much improved. There was already a local branch of Farmers' Institute for farm men, so through this channel Hoodless gained support for her idea, and the first Women's Institute was formed on 19 February 1897.

The purpose of this first group was to raise the standard of homemaking and health as well as to improve the intellectual and cultural life of rural women. Before long, other branches were formed and affiliation was established with Ontario's Department of Agriculture. Gradually over the next fifteen years, all provinces developed Women's Institutes.

Dr Cumming, principal of the Nova Scotia Agricultural College in Truro, initiated the movement in Nova Scotia, and the first Superintendent of Women's Institutes was Jennie Fraser, a native of New Glasgow and a home economics graduate of Macdonald College. The first Women's Institute began in Salt Springs, Pictou County, in July 1913; but by the end of the year, fourteen branches had been formed. The numbers grew rapidly, and through the next several decades Women's Institute became one of the most influential women's groups in the province.

The affiliation with the agricultural college and the provincial Department of Agriculture has continued to the present day, and the Women's Institutes of Nova Scotia (WINS) has its headquarters on the college's campus in Truro. Although the strength of W.I. has diminished in recent times, for many years the organization maintained great importance in the lives of rural women, due in part to the continuity of leadership provided by two long-reigning directors: Helen MacDougall and Norma Mosher.

Helen J. MacDougall, Director of WINS for twenty-five years and Director of Home Economics for the Department of Agriculture, was a woman of great energy and commitment. Through her planning and programming, domestic crafts such as quiltmaking and mat hooking were encouraged. She built on the skills and experience of the members and, through programs, demonstrations, and rallies, urged the exchange of pattern blocks and consideration of design and colour, while encouraging women to produce not only for their families but also for income.

In 1928, Handicraft Exchanges were set up throughout the province at strategic locations where WINS members were able to sell their hand-crafts to the public, particularly tourists travelling in the province. Con-

Busy Bee Sewing Group, Elderbank, Halifax County, 1940. Nova Scotia 4-H Council

sidered a success in its first couple of years of operation, this endeavour led the Department of Agriculture to create the Home Industries Division, a more ambitious marketing project, which promoted provincially made products both at home and further afield.

Also in 1928, the first Girls' Clubs were initiated by the department. These clubs were forerunners to 4-H and encouraged the continuation of quilting in the upcoming generation. Girls were given training in all the domestic arts, but most particularly sewing.

Women's Institute members both organized and entered quilting competitions, provincially and nationally. Working co-operatively with other organizations and government departments, WINS promoted the art and craft of quilting and encouraged women's economic development through the sale of quilts. W.I. groups also quilted for numerous charitable causes. Whether working for Red Cross overseas relief or helping in local disasters, WINS played a significant role in extending the tradition of quilting in Nova Scotia.

In the post-war period, through the 1950s to 1970s, Norma Mosher as director of WINS provided a second phase of continuous leadership, thereby maintaining the vitality and viability of WINS into more recent times. When the latest quilt revival of the 1970s began, WINS was able to provide leadership to new quilters who had not grown up in the tradition. At the same time, many experienced quilters were stimulated by the fresh injection of new ideas and techniques.

For a widow with eighteen children, even the weekly two-mile walk must have been a welcome change from the demands of home life. Quilting for the Red Cross may have been her only social outlet.

Red Cross

The story of WINS quilting runs parallel to the Red Cross quilting story. Beginning at approximately the same period, the Nova Scotia Division of the Canadian Red Cross Society opened in 1914, during the First World War. Many women's groups quilted, knitted, and made bandages and comforts for the Red Cross, but because of the excellent organization within WINS, the Red Cross was able to maximize efforts and production. Red Cross branches opened all over the province; often the very same people who quilted for WINS also worked in Red Cross groups. Some WINS groups operated essentially as local Red Cross branches during the First and Second World Wars, focusing their major efforts towards relief work.

While quilting for Red Cross was especially active during wartime, it was not restricted to those periods. When fires, droughts, or floods brought disaster, quilts were part of the relief aid. During the Great Depression of the 1930s, quilts were sent to the Prairies. In 1950, thousands of quilts went to flood victims in Manitoba. Nova Scotian women maintained very high production of quilts into the late 1960s, responding to calls for help from many countries in Africa, Asia, Europe, and South America.

In reviewing the Red Cross annual reports from the organization's beginning up until the present day, a remarkable record emerges. The records show that 43,323 quilts were sent overseas from Nova Scotia over the fifty-year period between 1915 and 1965; however, this does not amount to the sum total. There were years in which the statistical break-down between quilts and other bedding was not kept. Furthermore, the annual reports for the years 1938 to 1941 are missing. During the last four years of the Second World War alone, 25,149 quilts were shipped overseas. This does not reflect the thousands more quilts that were also made for local disaster relief, as well as for fundraising. Between 1955 and 1965, an average of 1,400 quilts a year were still being produced in Nova Scotia for Red Cross aid; two-thirds of those were sent overseas.[6]

Nova Scotia's Red Cross record is a further indication of the strength of the ongoing and continuous quilting tradition in Nova Scotia. It is also a testimony to the industry and generosity of the women of the province. Despite a relatively small population base (Nova Scotia over the years has averaged about four per cent of the total population of Canada), the output has been remarkable. During the floods in Britain and the Netherlands in 1953, of the 7,500 quilts sent from Canada, one-third were made by Nova Scotians. The province was consistently a high producer:

At the September 30 meeting, it was with great regret that Mrs J.J. Walsh's resignation was received. Mrs Walsh was Chairman of Women's Work for the Nova Scotia division for six years and during her term of office Nova Scotia led all other provinces in the manufacture of quilts for flood victims in Winnipeg, Holland and England.

Annual Report, 1954, Canadian Red Cross, Nova Scotia Division

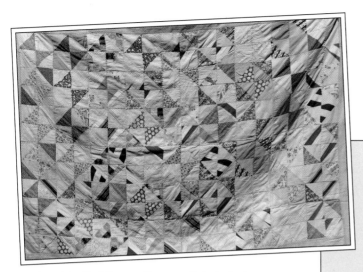

Canadian Red Cross quilt sent to Britain during World War II. Courtesy of Doreen Palmer, High Wycombe, England

Dear Red Cross

When I was a child in the Second World War I lived in Bath. My parents were given one of the quilts. It was very pretty.... I slept in a double bed with my sister and we had it on our bed. It kept us very warm and we had lots of fun making up stories about the different patterns. We used to wish we had dresses like the patterns. As well my brother was given a little all in one quilted suit like the anoracs we have today. All the other mothers around were in envy of him.

Back to the quilt. It had squares of about 6 inches and it was backed with some soft striped material and padded in between. We were very grateful to receive it and I have always remembered it. I wish I still had it now.

Yours sincerely,
Pat Staple

Letter from recipient of a Canadian Red Cross quilt, January 1992; courtesy of Pat Staple, Beachley, England

The opportunity to help in... connection with the 'World Refugee Year'.... I know you will be pleased to hear that what we have been asked to make are layettes and quilts. As most of you do this work, I feel sure we will have no difficulty to complete our extra quota of 250 layettes and quilts. If each branch and auxiliary does a few more than usual we will go 'over the top'. Of course our regular quota must be reached, too, so our other articles must be made as well.

Annual Report, 1959, Canadian Red Cross, Nova Scotia Division

Quilting for Manitoba Flood Relief, 1950; Society of Friends, Joggin Bridge, Digby County. Photo by John Collier, Jr.; Stirling County Study

Other Women's Groups

The Women's Institute was not the only organization to retain the quilting tradition. Many church groups quilted, some only occasionally and some on a regular basis.

They made quilts for various causes—to help local families in distress, for mission work, as gifts for ministers, as fundraisers, and, as might be expected, for the Red Cross. Some IODE (Imperial Order Daughters of the Empire) groups quilted during the war, as did numerous independent groups that were formed specifically to assist in the war relief effort. One such group in Oakland, Lunenburg County, was the War Workers Club. After the war, members changed the name to the Cosy Hour Club and continued meeting as a quilting group until the mid-1960s. Money made from the sale of quilts in the post-war years was donated to local charities.

Meeting of the Church of Christ Sewing Circle, Westport, Digby County, 1951. Photo by John Collier, Jr; Stirling County Study

Dauntless V Club, Truro, Colchester County, 1940s. "V for Victory" was a common slogan during the war. Photo by Alan Mosher; Colchester County Museum

Nova Scotia Industrial Exhibition, 1854
...this Exhibition shows that the females of our happier land are at liberty to spend their time, and display their ingenuity and taste, in pursuits better adapted to their sex, and in which it will be difficult to excel them. Who is there that can walk through our Assembly Room (in which, I take it for granted, after so genial an influence has been shed upon it,—we will never again hear the sounds of contention or of strife, (cheers and laughter,) without acknowledging that the success of the Exhibition must be attributed, after all, not so much to the men as to the women of Nova Scotia. (Loud cheers.)

Speech given by the Hon. William Young, Attorney General of Nova Scotia and member of the Executive Committee

Women might well have had something to do with the success of the exhibition; however, the orator was perhaps a little coy and misleading in his implication that Nova Scotian women were "at liberty" to pursue handwork as a pastime. Although fancy work was entered, the majority of items made by women and entered into the exhibit were practical, household essentials such as quilts, woven blankets and linens, rugs and carpets, homespun woolen cloth, and knitted goods.

"Nova Scotia Industrial Exhibition Building"
[Province House], Halifax, 1854. Lithograph,
drawn by G. Dubois; NSM 37.19

Exhibitions

Although women made quilts primarily for their own family use or for charitable purposes, exhibitions offered an opportunity for some to display their work publicly. Nova Scotia's earliest exhibition records are for the Exhibition of the Works of Industry of All Nations, held at the Crystal Palace, London, England, in 1851. The report on items from Nova Scotia mentions that "Quilts, blankets, woollen hearth-rugs, etc." were exhibited. While this report does not furnish us with any detail, the entry list for the first Nova Scotia Industrial Exhibition in Halifax in 1854 gives a better picture of the types of quilts on display during this period.

Nova Scotia Industrial Exhibition, 1854

Department 18 - Manufactures of Woolen, Linen & Cotton

#	Designation and Description...	Exhibitors Names and Residences
3	Wadded Quilts	Miss Mary Negus - S.E. Passage
18	Quilt	Mrs Patrick Whelan, Windsor
61	Bed Quilt	Mrs Duncan Grant, Musquodob't
77	Patchwork Quilt (silk)	Agnes Matthews, Halifax
89	Quilt	David McCurdy, Onslow
118	Patchwork Quilt	Catharine Himmelman, S.E. Passage
123	Quilt	Charitable Society, Yarmouth
131	Quilt	Mrs David Thompson, Porter's Lake
177	Quilt (Patchwork)	Charlotte Penny, Gay's River
185	Cotton Quilt	Angus McDonald, Douglas
189	Quilt	Mrs John Kelly, U. Stewiacke
199	Bed Quilt	Miss Sarah Burke, Liverpool
228	Silk Quilt	Miss Imlay, Halifax
235	Quilt	James Henderson, Truro
246	Quilt (Cotton)	Matilda O'Brien, Noel
253	Patchwork Quilt	Mrs James Norwood, Halifax
258	Bed Quilt	Miss Ellen Whiston, Halifax
273	Patchwork Quilt	Miss Hawthorn, Dartmouth
299	Quilt	Mrs J.P. Thompson, Hfx.
334	Patchwork Quilt	Mrs Marg't Burke, Windsor
347	Patchwork Quilt	Mrs Geo. Blanchard, Truro
354	Quilt, Cotton	Mrs Wiseman, Three Fathom Harbor
376	Bed Quilt	Miss Baillie, Annapolis *
393	Quilt, Patchwork	Mrs Thomson, Porter's Lake
394	Quilt & Hearthrug	Rob't McCurdy, Truro
395	Quilt, Patchwork	Miss Eliz'th McCulloch, Hfx.

420	Cotton Quilt	Mrs Wm. Fletcher, Truro
433	Bed Quilt	Mrs Thos. M. Crow, Truro
469	Bed Quilts - 2	Jno. P. Miller, Newport
475	Bed Quilt	Mrs Harvey, Newport
476	Bed Quilt	Mrs S. Logan, Gay's River
485	Quilt	Miss Reid, Musquodoboit
481	Quilt	Mrs Moshelle, Mahone Bay
505	Bed Quilts - two	Casper Eisner, Mahone Bay
523	Bed Quilt	Mrs W. Fletcher, Londonderry
533	Quilt	Mrs Meagher, Halifax
541	Quilt	Mrs Rob't McCurdy, Truro
567	Quilt	Miss Robertson, Barrington
580	Bed Quilt	Mrs McKenna, Lw'ceTown
605	Bed Quilt - Two	Syrena Donaldson, Liverpool
606	Bed Quilt	S. Mullins, Liverpool
612	Bed Quilt	Miss Frail, Cornwallis
614	Quilt	Mrs Wm. Young, Halifax

Department 26 - Fine Arts (Ladies' Department)

#	Designation and Description	Exhibitors Names and Residence
77	Quilt	Mrs B. Crow, Halifax
80	Silk Quilt	Mary Hanley, Halifax
91	Fancy Quilt	Mrs P. Whelan, Windsor
92	Do. Do. [ditto]	Mrs Wildman, Hfx.
132	Baby Quilt	Mrs Kennedy, Halifax
135	Silk Patchwork Table Cover	Mrs Willis Foster, Aylesford
161	Silk Patchwork Quilt	Mrs Jno. Pratt, Bridgetown
177	Child's Quilt	Mrs Robson, Pictou

The entry list includes other items described as knitted, crochet, netted, or Marseilles quilts; these have not been included here.

* Miss Baillie's patchwork quilt was made of 20,350 pieces!

*Quilts for sale at country fairs;
probably Lunenburg County, about 1910.
NSM 88.7.7, .8*

*The County Fair
On the other side of the building
were shown silk, worsted and
cotton patchwork quilts, wool
and linen counterpanes, hooked
mats, rag carpeting, knitted
socks and mittens, knitted and
crocheted quilts, woolen blankets
and gray and white yarn. The
articles shown here that were
most admired were two silk
quilts, one the work of Lettie
Freeman, the other a log cabin
design shown by Mrs P.
McGuire, of Lunenburg.*

*Bridgewater Bulletin,
14 October 1902*

Quilt displays have been a traditional part of agricultural fairs and county exhibitions for a long time and have continued to be a favourite attraction, both for quiltmakers and the general public.

Women's Institutes played a large part in promoting quilt displays and competitions. Local branches often were instrumental in the organization of fairs in their communities, and at provincial and national levels they sponsored many competitions and exhibitions. On 31 August 1927, the *Family Herald and Weekly Star* published an article on women's participation at the Canadian National Exhibition, Toronto. Both traditional and more modern handcrafts were displayed, and, because it was the sixtieth anniversary of Canadian Confederation, there were "such novelties as a case of 'confederation dolls', dressed in the costumes of 1867 and assembled at a quilting party". This historic tableau was meant to reflect the past. Urbanites at the time were especially caught up in nostalgia for bygone years and had been drawn into the latest quilt revival, promoted through women's periodicals and antique magazines. However, with the exception of period dress, the imagery expressed in the tableau was not far from the ongoing reality of many rural women in Nova Scotia and elsewhere who had never given up the tradition.

For some women, exhibitions were simply opportunities for displaying their skill and creativity with the needle. However, through the Women's Institute and later through the Handcrafts and Home Industries Division of the Nova Scotia Department of Industry and Publicity, women were also organizing exhibitions to advertise their crafts. As witnessed in their initiation of handicraft centres in the late 1920s, WINS was particularly interested in encouraging women to use their domestic skills for income generation.

Dear Sir,
Please find inclosed $ .25 entry
fee for one quilted aplique quilt—
Turkey red and white which I
am sending hope I have it done
Satisfactory. I made the desine
and did all the work myself. quilt
finished Aug. 11th, 1939.

I would like to have it put on
sale. Price $25.00 I did not put
the price on it as I was not sure
wether I should or not, as this is
my first experience in exhibiting
any thing So hope you will rectify
any mistakes.

I will not be able to be there to
look after the quilt and if not sold
please ret express charges collect
to...
Mrs Wm Cogswell
Centrville Kings Co N.S.

Thanking you very kindly
I remain yours truely

Mrs William Cogswell

Entry for the 1939 Nova Scotia
Provincial Exhibition; PANS

There is no record of
whether this quilt was sold,
but judging by what most
women were asking for their
quilts, this was a high price,
probably because it was
appliqué. In general, quilts
sold for $5 to $10.

During the 1920s and 1930s, individual efforts were also made to bring together design and traditional craft skills. One American designer, Eloise Steele, worked with Acadian women in the Pubnico area to produce saleable crafts, among them quilts and appliqué wall hangings.

By the 1940s and early 1950s, the Handcrafts Division of the government was organizing an annual Craftsmen-at-Work Exhibition in the province and also attended national and international trade shows. The division had professional craftspeople and designers on staff, and they worked in cooperation with the Women's Institute. Through talks and workshops on colour, design, and technique given to W.I. groups, division staff gave traditional needlewomen encouragement and ideas for creating marketable crafts that incorporated contemporary design elements.

One example of the experimental collaboration that occurred during the period between the Women's Institute and craftspeople affiliated with the Handcrafts Division was a pictorial 'stagecoach' quilt. It was designed by well-known Nova Scotian designer/craftsperson Winifred Fox and made by the Women's Institute, Coldbrook, Kings County; a photograph of it was included in the WINS publication, *Canadian Mosaic: Nova Scotia Volume*, 1957. Exhibited at the Craftsmen-at-Work Exhibition, it also won second prize in a 1952 quilt exhibition in Orillia, Ontario.

The Patchwork Quilt Business— here is a melancholy story of misspent time. The Yarmouth Herald in a notice of the recent county exhibition says:— Among the articles of female handiwork at the Fair, our attention was called to a quilt made by Miss Sarah Lovitt... which was composed of 182 squares, making together 13,104 pieces.... She commenced the quilt at age 11 and it was not completed until she was 15.

Colchester Sun, Truro, 31 October 1877

Not all journalists were appreciative of female handiwork. However, young Sarah may have the last laugh; over one hundred years later, a record of her work remains but Sarah's critic is lost to anonymity.

Competitions and Contests

Quilt competitions were not only organized by women's and craft groups. Newspaper and magazine contests also encouraged quilters to produce high-quality work. Prize money was considerably higher than the standard selling price of a quilt. With the additional possibility of public recognition, many quilters were enticed to enter. For example, Charlotte Scott, a woman from Hants County, won $100 in a *Toronto Star* contest during the 1950s. Her quilt was displayed in Eaton's department stores across Canada. In the *Star-Weekly* Dominion-wide Quilt-makers Contest in 1956, the Women's Institute of Pubnico, Yarmouth County, and a New Waterford woman won prizes of $250 each for the third best "Canadiana" quilt.[7]

Quilt History in Nova Scotia—Just the Beginning

Because the most recently made quilt in the museum exhibition dates from the 1950s, it seemed fitting for this text to bring the history of Nova Scotian quilts up to this time period. The 1950s also represent the last full decade of old-style quilting tradition; by the late 1960s the influences of the new wave were beginning to be felt, as is evident in the following quote:

> *Our first three books are on Quilting, which seems to be enjoying a revival in some quarters, although certainly it has never died out in Nova Scotia. Our chief complaint concerning some quilts we have seen is that the colours are frequently harsh in contrast and we would prefer to see some more subtle colouring; for instance, instead of using Paddy Green and Turkey Red on White, why not use Olive Green and Dull Gold, bringing them more into line with today's colours?*

> Handcrafts, April 1970, book review section,
> Handcrafts and Home Industries Division newsletter

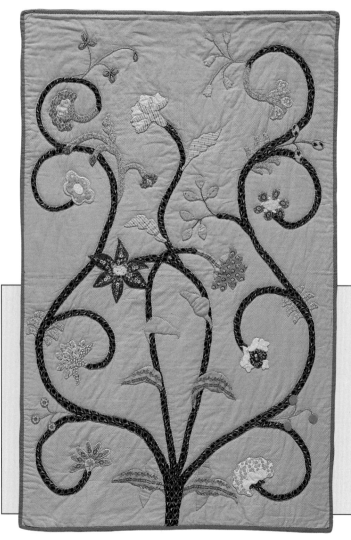

Using the 1950s as a watershed, the research for *Old Nova Scotian Quilts* focused on retrieving as much material as possible from the earliest records, primarily those in the public domain. Other sources have yet to be explored—diaries, letters, and documents that are privately owned. Furthermore, the oral accounts of older quilters would add immeasurably to our knowledge of quilting in the province as would accounts from family members who are still able to identify the makers of their heirloom quilts.

Finally, the quilts themselves have much to tell us. How were they made, and with what materials and patterns? Looking at these elements will help us to understand more about Nova Scotian quilts and the women who made them.

Appliqué picture, Tree of life, designed by Eloise Steele; made about 1935 by Acadian women, Centre East Pubnico, Yarmouth County
53 x 82 cm (21˝ x 32¼˝)
NSM 55.18

This piece was exhibited in the 1945 Craftsmen-at-Work Exhibition in Halifax. Fabrics from the mid-1800s found in local attics were used for flowers, stems, and leaves. The 'tree of life' design was derived from printed fabric imported from India in the late 1700s.

CHAPTER 3

Sewing, Equipment, and Fabric

Top →
Filler →
Back →

In Britain, women have quilted and made patchwork for well over three hundred years.

For my part I have plyed my needle these fifty years, and by my good will would never have it out of my hands.... I have quilted counterpanes and chest covers in fine white linen, in various patterns of my own invention. I have made patchwork beyond calculation.

Letter from a Miss Hulton to the *Spectator*, 1700; quoted in Miall, 1937

What Is a Quilt?

Today, a quilt is often described as a 'fabric sandwich' of three layers—top, filler, and back. These layers are usually held together by lines of quilting stitches; in some examples, tying replaces quilting. For convenience and by long usage, the term 'quilt' also includes several types that are not actually quilted or do not contain a filler, such as crazy quilts and many log cabin quilts.

Searching through historical documents, it soon becomes apparent that the word 'quilt' was used loosely in the past, perhaps simply meaning 'bedding'. For instance there are many references to 'quilts' which have a modifier such as 'woven' or 'knitted'. This broad usage continues today in some families who ask their children to 'get under the quilts' when going to bed, even if the bedding is blankets.

Traditionally, quilts were bedcoverings designed to be viewed on a bed (which influenced placement of pattern and border). In a modern context, 'quilt' includes other forms, some of which are intended to be viewed on the wall. Fine artists as well as quiltmakers now employ piecing and quilting techniques, and their work stretches the definitions of what a quilt is and what it can become. Through exploration and exchange, traditional quilters are encouraged to consider and employ new methods in the construction and ornamentation of their quilts.

In Canada and the United States, the term 'quilting' really means quiltmaking and includes both the making of the top—the piecing or appliqué—and the stitching together of the three layers. For convenience, quilts are subdivided into groups according to the construction method used to make the top—pieced, log cabin, crazy, wholecloth, and appliqué. It seems that past quilters in Nova Scotia did not categorize their work. They often described pieced and appliqué quilts as simply 'patchwork' or 'my quilting'.

In Britain there is a practical separation of the two major aspects of quiltmaking—patchwork and quilting. When interest in quilting was revived in Britain in the 1930s, little attention was paid to patchwork,[1] and in the books by Elizabeth Hake and Agnes Miall,[2] and later by Mavis FitzRandolph and others,[3] the patterns of the quilting stitches continued to be of greater importance.

Materials

The only materials needed to make a quilt are cloth, thread, and batting. However, within this small list of required materials, considerable variety exists. Necessity rather than choice often dictated whether a quilter used new or recycled material. Wool and cotton were the most common quilt fabrics, but silk and velvet were also used for fancier work. Flax was grown in Nova Scotia, so it may be that linen was at one time more commonly used; only one quilt in the museum collection (Q 18) has a linen backing. Sewing thread was generally cotton, but sometimes the quilting thread was of the same fibre as the cloth in wool or silk quilts.

Quilters proved themselves to be very resourceful when it came to selecting filler material. As might be expected, the usual filler was cotton or wool batting. However, inside some quilts can be found older, worn-out quilts. Of the quilts illustrated here, two have quilt fillers (Q 18, 19), and one (Q 34) was discovered as the filler inside another quilt. Blankets, burlap, and old clothing have also been found in older quilts in the province. One woman recalls seeing a quilt with newspaper as the filler.[4] This idea may not be as odd as it sounds:

Paper Bed Clothes—As there is much cause for fear that the winter may be long and severe, and as from the very general distress at this time the call on the charitable for food, apart from that of clothing, for the poor will be great, a correspondent thinks it as well to point out that much additional warmth may be obtained by a covering of paper between the bed-clothes. Doubtless to many this may appear absurd, but a few words will show its correctness, and at such a time a cheap means for additional warmth may be useful to many. A blanket is not in itself warmer than a sheet; it merely retains the heat given off from the body, while the sheet allows it to pass freely off. A covering therefore, of any material must tend to produce warmth in accordance with the degree in which it retains heat or permits the passage of it, and that paper is, more or less, a non-conductor of heat is certain and proved by the simple fact that in taking hold of the hot handle of a vessel, the hand may be protected from the heat by even a thin covering of paper, whereas one of metal, linen or cotton of the same thickness, would be almost useless. It is thus evident a paper is a non-conductor of heat in a great degree. Brown paper of 4½ or 5 feet may be easily procured and cost but little, and a sheet of such paper, or even old newspapers, placed between the upper bedclothes would give some increase of warmth where an extra blanket is not obtainable.

The Presbyterian Witness, 8 February 1879

Pieced quilt top, four-patch and sixteen-patch blocks; fabrics from the 1850s, probably Yarmouth County; NSM 78.49.2

Women and children at Clark's Harbour, Shelburne County, late 1800s. Many of these dress fabrics probably ended up in quilts. Photo by William Brannen

Nothing Wasted–Cotton Sacks in Quiltmaking

Much has already been written by quilt historians[5] on the use of cotton sacks in quiltmaking. The sacks were originally produced to hold flour, salt, sugar, and feed. Recycling them for use in quilts, clothing, and other articles was common practice throughout North America, and Nova Scotia was no exception.

Such recycling was both necessary and encouraged, particularly during the 1920s, '30s, and '40s. Feed companies responded to the demand in various ways: sometimes they gave instructions on removing the lettering; sometimes they had the lettering on separate paper bands that could be taken off. Sacks with coloured prints were also popular as they could be used for many sewing projects.

Suggestions on how to remove the ink lettering from the sacks were published in several local newsletters. In a 1949 *Home and Country* newsletter, Women's Institute members were given five different methods.

Writer and broadcaster Helen Dacey Wilson grew up in Guysborough County during the 1930s. She describes how the use of flour sacks could make things difficult for young girls:

Perhaps the practical idea we hated most was my mother's clever uses for flour and sugar bags.... Mama used to bleach these bags out and use them for pillowcases, white aprons for herself, shirts for the boys, and, most hated of all, for petticoats and bloomers for the girls. They were all right after they had been worn and washed many times, but the first bleachings never took all the lettering off–just dimmed down all the messages and instructions.

I remember one day my sister Elsie just refused to go to school because the nurse was coming and Elsie's flour-bag slip and sugar-bag bloomers were new and had not yet faded completely.... On the back of her petticoat the words CREAM OF THE WEST could be clearly seen—and a large still bright blue arrow pointing to the words UNTIE HERE stood out plainly on the seat of her bloomers.

Grete told me that she remembers being invited to a cousin's house... and the group decided to go swimming. Grete loved swimming and wanted to go too, but she couldn't bear the thought of undressing with the others. Before leaving home she had counted <u>four</u> messages on her underwear, and that was too much for any girl to stand.

More Tales from Barrett's Landing,
Toronto: McClelland & Stewart, 1967

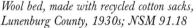

West Hants—A splendid exhibit and talk on "Flour Bag Possibilities" was then given by Mount Denson Institute.... Ladies' and children's garments, pillow cases, sheets, nightgowns, quilts, aprons, luncheon sets and handkerchiefs were shown. All these were made from flour, feed or salt bags... a very attractive exhibit showing skill and thrift....

Home and Country, September 1930, newsletter, Women's Institute of Nova Scotia

Wool bed, made with recycled cotton sacks, Lunenburg County, 1930s; NSM 91.18

Myrna Wentzell spring cleaning, Riverport, Lunenburg County, about 1920. Photo by Roy Creaser; courtesy of the Fisheries Museum of the Atlantic, NSM neg. N-18,166

Doulan farm, Grand Lake, Cape Breton County, 1913; Beaton Institute, UCCB. Note the quilt on the fence.

Eaton's catalogue, 1927. The vacuum clothes washer was referred to by one local man in the 1970s as a 'quilt stomper', the term his mother had used.

Mary Elizabeth (Wood) Smith; Beaton Institute, UCCB

Washday—Making Them 'Soft and New'

Today we think of old quilts as rather precious and consider carefully how to clean and conserve them. However, our great-grandmothers did not regard their everyday quilts as delicate artifacts. A quilt was made to be used. When it became well worn, it could possibly end up as upholstery padding, bedding for the dog or, finally, rag scraps.

This helpful hint appeared in the *Presbyterian Witness* on 21 September 1889: "If quilts are folded or rolled tightly after washing, then beaten with a rolling-pin or potato-masher, it lightens up the cotton and makes them soft and new." Modern-day conservators would shudder, but this was probably not considered an extreme method for handling quilts.[6]

Most women washed and aired their bedding at least once in the spring and again in the fall, a chore not without its pleasures. The satisfaction in seeing the results of one's work is evident in this diary entry:

Friday Nov br 20th [1891]
a verry fine day Lewis ploughing GP banking the house Mrs Brown hear washing woolen clothes and Blankets Flora and Sarah and Bella helping her I spinning... the cotton clothes that was put out yesterday are lovely and dry we left them out last night they have got them all in nice and dry and the bushes and fences full of blankets and quilts and woolen clothes of every discription and cotton dress and all sorts.

The writer, Mary Elizabeth (Wood) Smith (1812-1892), lived in Inverness County, Cape Breton, with her son and his family. Her diary is an excellent source of information about day-to-day work on a farm. She was 79 when she wrote the above entry, and she continued to write and be an active participant in the family chores until her death the following year.

Equipment

In spite of the addition of more modern tools such as rotary cutters and various types of markers for transferring quilting designs to cloth, the basic tools for quiltmaking have remained unchanged. Scissors, thimble, needles, and quilt frame and clamps have always been essential, and sometimes homemade templates for cutting and marking were used.

Finding written reference to such ordinary implements is very rare; however, in the inventory of Capt. Robert Wirling of Shelburne, dated 1800, a quilting frame was listed. It was valued at five shillings.

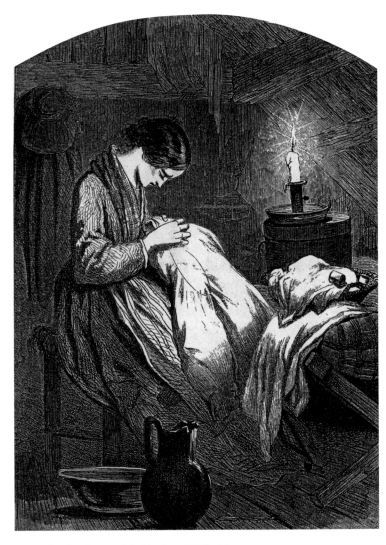

"The Old Sewing Machine" and *"The New Sewing Machine"*. Godey's Lady's Book, Philadelphia, January and March 1863

Sewing Machines

The introduction of the home sewing machine in the 1850s made a major change in the world of sewing. Many projects could be completed in far less time than if done by hand. In spite of this, the impact that the sewing machine had on quiltmaking was limited. In Nova Scotia, most quilters continued to piece by hand. Quite a few quilts in the museum collection contain some machine sewing, usually to piece larger sections of the quilt top, to seam fabric for the backing, or to apply the binding. The stems on Q 30 and the frames around the portraits on Q 46 are the only examples in this collection of appliqué done by machine. No quilt is machine quilted.

With all its practicality, the sewing machine did not necessarily provide women with the pleasure and pride that could come from doing fine handwork and, as far as sociability was concerned, it could not compete with the quilting party.

Sewing machines in Halifax, about 1870. Photos by Joseph S. Rogers; NSM 80.104

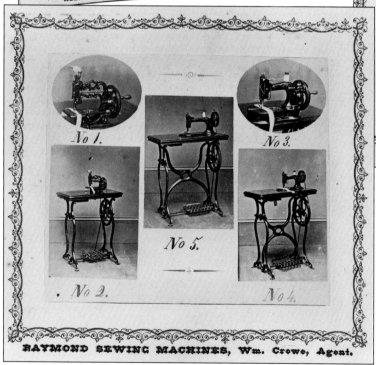

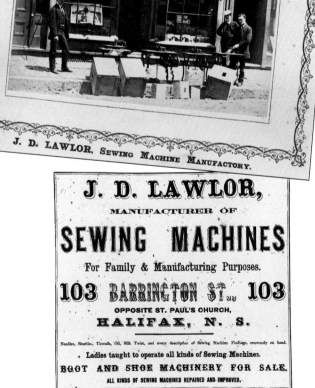

Quilt block, 'sunflower'; NSM 92.34.5
The pieces are assembled and applied by machine.
Blanket-stitch embroidery around the edges of
appliqué became popular in the early 1900s.

Pattern Blocks

As will be discussed more thoroughly in the next section on patterns and patterning, most quilts were not entirely original in their design. Quilters began with traditional patterns, often improvising to create personal variations. Although patterns were published in magazines and newspapers, many women acquired designs from family and friends. To remember an appealing pattern a woman might stitch up a rough block as a note to herself; with the accumulation of time, she could develop quite a collection. The Nova Scotia Museum has two significant collections of pattern blocks, one from Annapolis County, the other from Yarmouth County. Each collection was started by one woman, then handed down and added to by at least one if not two generations.

Pattern blocks, about 1900 to 1930s,
Carleton, Yarmouth County; NSM 73.30.1+
There are 27 blocks in this collection.
Mrs Hilton (died 1954) added the notations
and may have made some of the blocks. Others
were acquired from her mother or another older
quilter. Pieced quickly out of scraps, they were
made only to record designs.

CHAPTER 4

Patterns and Patterning

Detail of Q_18

*P*eople in all cultures have developed patterns to ornament practical things. Cloth, containers, tools, buildings, and interiors are decorated more to satisfy the eye and the spirit than to assist function. Pattern in the broadest sense is an important part of our lives and appears nearly everywhere, even in the way we arrange plates on a shelf, ornaments on a mantel, and pictures on a wall. It organizes routine activity, speech, music, and dance. Pattern in quilts uses motifs that are repeated, changed, and developed to create variations and new ideas.

Over the years, most quilters in Nova Scotia have maintained traditional designs in preference to personal invention, because familiar patterns and approaches are more comfortable. However, working within the restrictions of traditional patterns or styles, quiltmakers have created imaginative and often striking variations.

Origins of Patterns

Independently, many cultures conceived of the same fundamental shapes of circle and square, as well as basic subdivisions of these shapes, especially right-angle triangles. Therefore, it is impossible to attribute to any particular cultural group the origins of the simplest geometric shapes such as those found in quilts.

As well, the tradition of making patchwork can not be traced to a single origin. Piecing, or joining together of shapes to create patterns, occurs in cultures throughout America, Asia, Europe, and Africa. Appliqué as a decorative technique is known around the world.

Because of the general history of traditional quilts in Nova Scotia, we assume that most of the approach to patterning derives from British or American roots. However, other groups may also have contributed to the development of quiltmaking in ways that we cannot yet identify. Clues may come from examining the smallest details of construction. The pattern a quiltmaker chooses may be influenced by other women in a community or by available publications, but evidence of her cultural origin may be retained in the style of finish or in colour combinations. In Nova Scotia, such details have yet to be recorded and analysed as part of the search for cultural influences.

Technique

One characteristically British technique is the use of paper templates to piece patterns; this is distinct from the North American approach to pattern assembly. On this side of the Atlantic, the paper template technique was used almost exclusively to make silk hexagon or diamond designs in the Victorian period, although earlier examples in cotton are known here (Q 2), when traditions were closer to their British roots. Many people in Britain still use this traditional paper method, even to make quilts based on American patterns.[1] However, if a British quiltmaker follows all the instructions for piecing and finishing given in an American book, it may be difficult to distinguish her quilt from North American examples.

Detail of Q 2

Another example is the old British style of finishing quilts—the edges were joined with a single line of running stitch through all layers, after front and back material were both turned inward. Sometimes a binding tape was included in this process (Q 44). In North America, the edge is usually bound with another strip of cloth sewn to the front and turned to the back and attached (both raw edges of the binding cloth are also turned inward). Occasionally, no binding strip was used, but the front fabric or back fabric (Q 4) itself is folded over the edge of the quilt and sewn down, with the raw edge turned.

Naming of Quilt Patterns

Quilt patterns may have local names, but very few have been recorded. Most quilters use 'standard' late-twentieth-century names, which derive largely from the wealth of American publications. In this book and exhibition, identification generally follows that usage. In the museum's collection, only a few quilts were acquired with the pattern name used by the maker. One in particular is a quilt actually inscribed with the title of 'Star of Bethlehem' and the date '1925' in pencil (Q 25). Others were named through family oral tradition and relayed to the museum by descendants.

Nine-patch block, late 1800s, Yarmouth County; NSM 73.30.4

In the past, quilters did not always use names for the patterns. Ada Walfield referred only to her 'patchwork quilt', although the pattern here is described as a 'triple nine-patch' (Q 10). To describe the set of another quilt (Q 19), she used a local term, 'herringbone', rather than the usual 'zig-zag' or 'rail fence'. Similarly, the name 'fisherman's reel' which accompanied one quilt (Q 22) seems more suited to this coastal province than the names 'fox and geese' or 'double X' found in published sources.

Nova Scotians now use standard quilting terminology; only a few distinctive words have been observed in scattered usage. For example, the word 'hung' was used by one quilter to describe placing square blocks at 45° to the edge of the quilt (Q 13, 18, 19, 20, 22), but use of this term is not general.[2]

If old terms are still used in specific regions of the province, it would be valuable to record them before they are completely replaced by imported words. As the scope of this project did not include the collecting of oral history, this subject has not been explored. We do know that there are local terms used in Acadian communities of the region. Instead of 'courtepointe' for quilt, Acadians often say 'couverte piquée' or simply 'couverte'. Instead of 'la corvée à piquer' for 'quilting party', in south-western Nova Scotia a common term is 'la coultine'. In other parts of Acadia 'le frolic à piquer' is used.

Patterns for Piecing–Simple Geometry

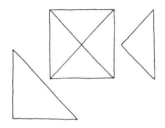

Although there is no written evidence, the quilts themselves demonstrate that early quilters understood basic geometry. Patterns of most pieced quilt blocks are easily figured out by an experienced quilter who can interpret the structure of the design. Almost all patterns for early Nova Scotian pieced quilts are made with two basic geometric shapes—squares and right-angle triangles.

Squares and Triangles

The most elementary pattern results when many small squares are sewn together, as in the 'postage stamp' design (Q 6). Because all the units are the same, there is no variation possible except through colour.

To create repeating patterns, most quilts are built up with geometric shapes in square pattern block units. These square units combine easily in multiples to produce a quilt top which is square or rectangular, adaptable to any size of bed.

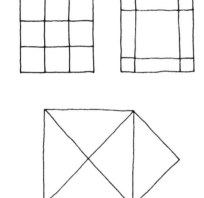

One of the simplest arrangements subdivides the pattern block into smaller squares, producing 'double Irish chain' (Q 7), for example. But the 'nine-patch' is the most common traditional pattern block made with squares. There are two main variations: in the first there are nine equal squares (centre of Q 10); in the second, the central square is larger, surrounded by the other eight, looking like a picture frame (see Q 8, 9, 10).

A square can also be subdivided into right-angle triangles. It is important to recognize that either two or four triangles will combine to make a square. In both cases, although the squares are not the same size, the triangles are identical in shape.

Together, squares and right-angle triangles produce a broad range of patterns, such as 'rob Peter to pay Paul' (Q 11), 'pinwheel' (Q 15), 'flying geese' (Q 14), or 'fisherman's reel' (Q 22).

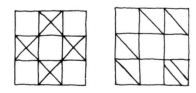

As well, right-angle triangles and squares can be used to fill a nine-patch grid. With shadings in light and dark, there are many possibilities (Q 12, 13, 18, 20, 23). A quiltmaker sees through the pattern in a simple quilt block to the structure of the grid that underlies it. With an understanding of the grid, it is easier to observe that many patterns are closely related.

Diamonds and Hexagons

The next most common shape used in quilt patterns is a diamond. At first, all diamonds seem the same, but there are two forms. When several are assembled into a star motif, the difference is clear. Diamonds with 45° and 135° angles produce an eight-pointed star (Q 25, 27, 28). Diamonds with 60° and 120° angles produce a six-pointed star (Q 29), or three will form a hexagon (Q 26).

The hexagon shape, and the 60°/120° diamond as a subdivision of it, can be drawn accurately with only a compass (or a pin and thread) and a pencil to scribe a circle. The radius of any size of circle will always divide the circumference into six parts, producing a hexagon when the crossings are connected with straight lines. No protractor or special instrument is required.

In old Nova Scotian quilts, the hexagon appears most often in patchwork related to English tradition (Q 2). The only common hexagon pattern in North America is called 'grandmother's flower garden'.

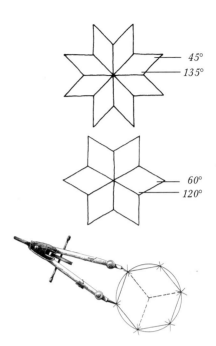

45°
135°

60°
120°

The Dictionary of Needlework,
S. Caulfeild & B. Saward, London,
1887 edition

Hexagon pieces, made about 1860,
Uniacke family, Mount Uniacke,
Hants County; NSM 49.9.30

To piece silk cloth and keep all the angles accurate, the quilter often used a paper pattern, cut to the exact shape, behind each piece of cloth. In Nova Scotia, this English method of piecing with paper was used primarily for silk patchwork and hexagon patterns.

Doll's pieced quilt, made about 1930
44 x 69 cm (17¼˝ x 27˝); NSM Z4357

From Quilt Patterns *catalogue,*
Ladies Art Company, St. Louis,
Missouri, 1928; NSM 91.100.7

Other Shapes

Other geometric shapes, such as lozenges, equilateral triangles, rhomboids, and other shapes seen in British patchwork, are not noted in Nova Scotian pieced quilts.

When complex geometric patterns are seen, they can often be traced to a published design. In the early 1900s, local women saved newspaper columns and advertisements for quilt patterns in their scrapbooks for later reference. Columns appeared in the *Maritime Farmer*, the *Family Herald*, and other newspapers and magazines. Almost all of these were syndicated columns that presented traditional American designs (and variations) or new patterns by contemporary designers. One of the best known designers was Ruby Short McKim; her book *One Hundred and One Patchwork Patterns* was first published in 1931, but her patterns were published in Canada at least as early as 1928 in *Chatelaine* magazine.

Mary (Seaman) Pike moved to Arcadia, Yarmouth County, in 1874 where her husband served as a minister for four years. Shortly after arriving, Mary wrote to her mother in Minudie, Cumberland County, and described the parsonage in some detail. This excerpt gives an indication that not all quilts were simple in design:

You ought to see some of the pillow slips, how they are tucked, etc, and the patchwork of some of the quilts I think would puzzle even Grandmother Seaman....

Seaman family correspondence, July 1874; courtesy of Ruth Symes

Patterns for Sets

Complex arrangements for sets were not used in the province, but several standard arrangements are observed frequently in traditional pieced quilts. In the two most straightforward, the pattern block is placed either next to another pattern block, or next to a set block. The pattern-to-pattern approach often produces incidental designs where the blocks touch, adding greater visual complexity and interest to the overall pattern (Q 11, 15, 21, 30, 49). The alternating pattern and set approach tends to isolate the motifs.

Using *two* alternating pattern blocks creates other possibilities, but this approach is not common except for a few well-established old favourites (Q 7, 12, 13).

In another common set, squares and rectangles form a frame around the blocks (Q 8, 9, 10, 22). This is called 'sash' or 'window sash'.

A less common set arrangement is the diagonal placement of square blocks, described as 'hung' or 'tipped'. This 'tipped' placement gives diagonal movement to the squares, creating a more dynamic visual presentation (Q 14, 18, 19, 20, 22). In some patterns, diagonal movement is already part of the design, and blocks do not have to be tipped (Q 7, 10, 12, 17, 23, 30, 31).

With a little ingenuity, this diagonal placement is turned into 'herringbone' set (Q 18, 19). It is visually related to the 'hung' arrangement, except that the set block becomes two triangles, and these are slipped so the tip of one aligns with the middle of its neighbour. This set seems to occur most commonly in Lunenburg County. It is also found in the United States, especially Pennsylvania, where it is known as 'streak of lightning' or 'rail fence'. As Pennsylvania and Lunenburg were both settled by Germanic people, there could be a common root for this design.

In Nova Scotia, few quilts have borders. When used, they were often just plain frames (Q 7). No appliqué swag borders or other fancy motifs found in American examples have been seen here.

Patterns for Appliqué

In Nova Scotia, appliqué quilts are far less common than pieced quilts. Judging from a few examples, old designs tended to be rather straightforward. Most employ a repeating pattern block (Q 49), sometimes with a set block. Another arrangement favours nine blocks surrounded by a vine border (Q 50). A few present a single large motif, such as the idiosyncratic 'snowflake' (Q 48). After 1900, appliqué patterns became more popular through published sources (Q 47), but traditional pieced favourites have always predominated.

Detail of Q 27

Patterns for Quilting

Like the pieced and appliqué patterns chosen by Nova Scotians in the 1800s and early 1900s, the quilting patterns also tended to be direct and practical. Of course there are wonderful exceptions in the elaborate wholecloth quilts (Q 40, 41, 42, 43), but in the numerous pieced quilts, the quilting was simple.

For ordinary quilts, often only enough quilting was done to keep the filler from shifting. This is especially true for wool beds (Q 3). With minimal quilting, a wool bed could be taken apart easily for cleaning. The interior wool batt was washed separately, then recarded to fluff it up for extra warmth. The reassembled layers were held in place with tied yarn or widely spaced stitches.

Pieced quilts with cotton batts were quilted more closely, with the stitching directly related to the pattern of the top. One common approach was to quilt on both sides of each seam of the squares and triangles in the design (Q 10, 12, 13, 18, 19, 22, 25, 26). Single or crossed lines, sometimes diagonal, were commonly used to fill larger areas of plain fabric (Q 14, 20); frequently these connect the corners of the pattern shapes (Q 6, 7, 9, 49).

Intricate quilting motifs were reserved for the showiest of white/ wholecloth quilts. They did not appear on pieced quilts until the 1900s when commercial patterns and quilt batt wrappers supplied ornate designs to fill spaces in pieced quilts (Q 27); these were printed by the Dominion Wadding Company, Montreal, as well as by Stearns & Foster and other American firms. Many Nova Scotian quilters continued to use straight lines (Q 28) or substituted simpler motifs.

In some quilts, the quilting lines totally ignore the carefully made pieced or appliqué design. Such is the case with the 'snowflake' appliqué quilt (Q 48) where crossing diagonal lines create a waffle pattern without any reference to the snowflake design. This lack of relationship between design elements is seen elsewhere, too. For example, in Northern Ireland perhaps 80 per cent of quilts, regardless of design, are quilted all-over with rows of angled chevrons, which is called 'wave' quilting there.[3]

Arrangement of Colours and Tones

Another aspect of basic design in old quilts is the careful arrangement of mixed fabrics. Many makers could not afford new cloth for quilts, but they often achieved remarkable results with left-over scraps. More than by colour, fabrics were sorted according to light and dark tones (Q 6, 7, 8, 9, 10, 20). Sometimes they were sorted in three tones—dark, medium, and light (Q 26). Red, strategically placed, was often used for bold accent (Q 10, 25, 27, 33).

In some patterns, the placement of colours was dictated by the design; for instance, pieced or appliqué elements such as flowers and green leaves were always interpreted literally (Q 30, 45, 47, 49, 50). In most geometric pieced quilt patterns, colours could be chosen freely. Occasionally, commercially printed patterns such as 'broken star' (Q 27) indicated which colours to use and where to place them, but some quilters still made their own choices.

Detail of Q 26

CHAPTER 5

A Gallery of Quilts
From the Nova Scotia Museum Collection

*T*he following gallery of old Nova Scotian quilts presents a wide range, from the most basic, functional bedcovers to highly decorative examples of needlework skill, more to be admired than used. Quilters from the humblest circumstances share honour with more affluent makers, for their work is a valuable legacy. Studying these quilts and learning about the women who made them not only extends our knowledge of the tradition but also adds to our appreciation of the lives of the quiltmakers, and of the caring, creativity, and history embodied in their work.

The Oldest Quilts Known in Nova Scotia

The contrast between humble and affluent is exemplified by these two quilts. They illustrate differences in how people lived in the province in the early 1800s. Settlers in rural areas often produced homespun woolen cloth, while people in garrisons and towns had access to imported goods.

Pieced quilt

Four-patch

made about 1810,
probably in the
Johnson family,
Collingwood,
Cumberland County

wool; 168 x 188 cm (66″ x 74″)
NSM 67.127.57

Construction

Pieces in this quilt top are home-spun, handwoven woolen cloth saved from worn clothing and recycled. The maker created a simple repeating pattern in spite of limited resources, with up to seven scraps sewn together to make one patch; each four-patch pattern block measures about 28 cm (11″). Worsted wool thread was used to quilt lines 3 to 4 cm apart (1¼″ to 1½″).

History

This a rare survival–people do not usually save such common-place things. It arrived at the museum as a packing blanket wrapped around a more precious item of furniture. Ironically, the quilt now holds much greater prominence in the collection as a valuable cultural artifact.

Pieced quilt top

Hexagons

*made about 1810,
probably Halifax*

cotton
192 x 238 cm (75½″ x 93¾″)
NSM 84.23

Construction

The stitches that baste each piece of cloth to a paper pattern still remain because the sewing project was never completed. Therefore, the unfaded dress and furnishing fabrics are excellent examples of what was used at that time. The hexagon pieces were assembled with fine sewing, about 8 to 10 stitches per cm (18 to 20 per inch).

History

The unknown maker was presumably someone with leisure time who had access to an array of fancy imported cottons, many of which date from the late 1700s.

Detail of the reverse: The template paper was cut from Nova Scotian newspapers and a hardware catalogue, as well as from handwritten letters. Several advertisements for Halifax merchants are dated between 1802 and 1805.

Wool Beds

Wool beds are also known in different parts of Nova Scotia as tied quilts, puffs, or comfortables. Such bedding could be either quilted with large stitches or tied. For extra warmth, a wool bed was sometimes used on top of the mattress, too.

Wool for quilt batts could be carded by hand, but carding machines in mills produced much larger sheets of wool batting.

Cotton batting was imported from the United States.

Wile Carding Mill, Bridgewater. Exterior, 1888; interior, 1991

Wool bed

made in the late 1800s, Amherst, Cumberland County, or New Minas, Kings County

wool; 171 x 172 cm (67¼" x 67¾") NSM 75.119

Construction

This quilt was made with a thick wool batt and two woolen blankets, probably handwoven. The blankets were hemmed individually, then joined along the edges to contain the batt. Using large stitches, the quilting pattern consists of crossed lines about 20 cm (8") apart.

Pieced Quilts

Known as patchwork in earlier times, pieced quilts make up the largest grouping of old quilts in Nova Scotia.

Fabric scraps are sewn together in blocks, which are then assembled, with or without a set, to make a quilt top. In most old quilts in the province, the pattern goes out to the edges; wide borders were rarely used.

Pieced quilt

Rectangles

*made about 1880,
probably Lunenburg County*

*wool
167 x 226 cm (65¾ ˝ x 89˝)
NSM 73.379.2*

Construction

Cut from previously patched clothing, the irregular rectangles were assembled in strips. A heavy wool batt made this rudimentary bedcover very warm. Quilted lines 5 to 7 cm apart (2 to 2 ¾˝) form a chevron pattern, with linen and some woolen thread. To finish the side edges, the selvage of the backing fabric was brought to the front, while at top and bottom, the edges were turned in.

Pieced quilt

Strip

*made about 1900,
probably in the
MacKenzie family,
Scotsburn,
Pictou County*

*cotton
192 x 197 cm
(75½″ x 77½″)
NSM 92.84.1*

Construction

Because the design of this quilt is so
basic, the most outstanding feature is the
patterned quilting.

Strip quilts were made more commonly
in Britain than in Nova Scotia.

Pieced quilt

Inch or postage stamp

possibly 1860s, marked "Maggie C. Chesley", Bridgetown, Annapolis County

cotton
187 x 198 cm
(73½″ x 78″)
NSM 72.313

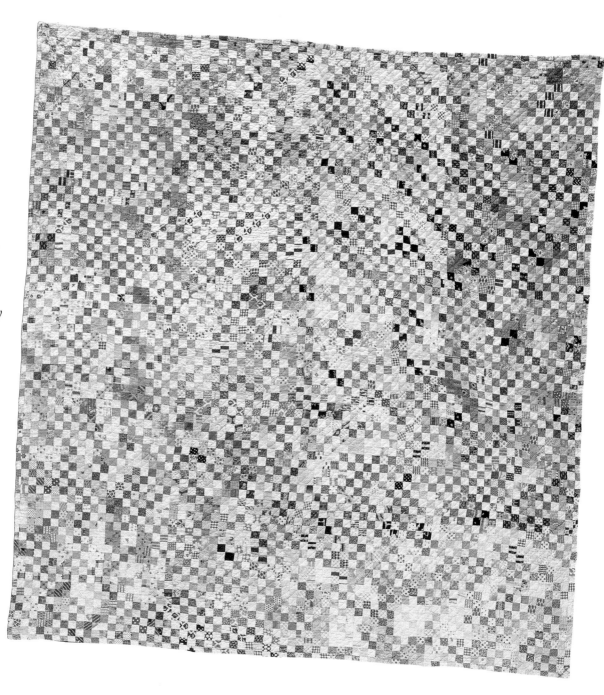

Construction

The quilt top is made of 5,467 one-inch squares! In addition, some squares are made of two or three pieces, using the tiniest scraps. Dozens of different cotton prints were sorted into lights and darks, creating a checkerboard effect.

Simple quilted lines pass through the corners of each square. The edge was finished in an unusual way: a strip of pink cloth was sewn to the front, then turned to the back side, without showing on the top.

History

Maggie Chandlish Chesley (born 1845) was probably the maker and may have pieced the quilt as a lesson in sewing when she was young.

Pieced quilt

Double Irish chain

made about 1890,
probably Clementsport,
Annapolis County

cotton
184 x 236 cm (72½″ x 93″)
NSM 74.69.2

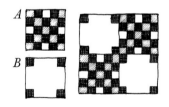

Construction

This well-known pattern is made of two alternating basic units: block A is composed of 25 small squares sewn together to make a large block; block B is one large white square with four small squares at the corners (sewn on top of the basic square).

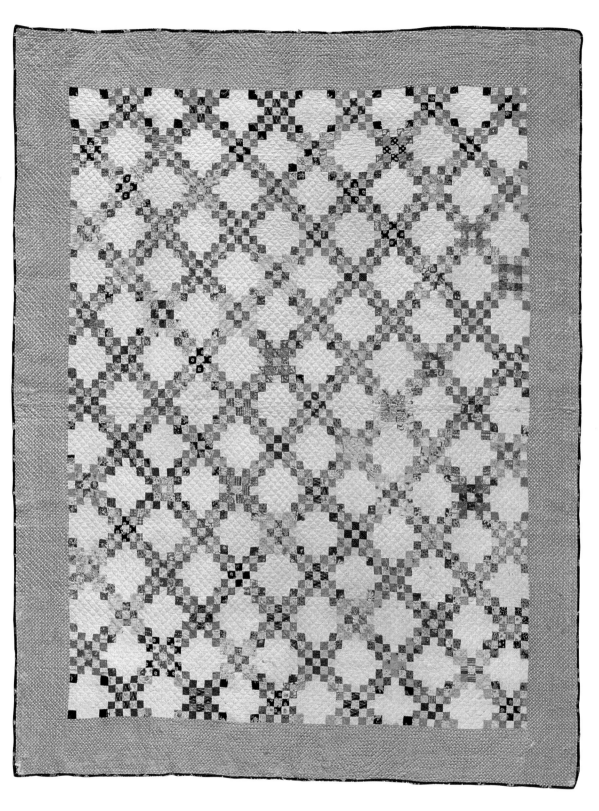

Pieced quilt

Nine-patch

*made about 1900,
probably Yarmouth County*

cotton
161 x 202 cm (63¼˝ x 79½˝)
NSM 74.361.3

Construction

Set with a lighter printed material, the blocks appear to float on the background. The blocks are not connected by corner squares in the set, as they are in Q 9, 10.

Pieced quilt

Nine-patch

*made about 1900,
probably Lunenburg County*

cotton
160 x 192 cm (63˝ x 75½˝)
NSM 74.381.5

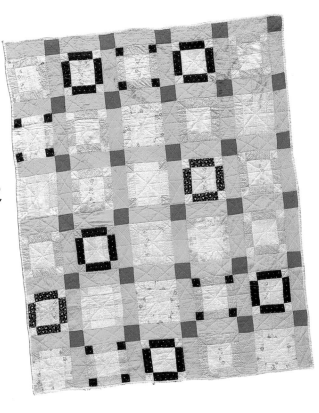

Nine-patch blocks

Nine-patch blocks are very common in traditional Nova Scotian quilts.

These are the two basic forms.

Many other patterns are based on nine-patch grids.

With the blocks 'hung', red triangles between the outer row of dark reddish nine-patch blocks give the impression of a framing border. This attractive variation has not been noted in other old quilts in the province. Windsor, Hants County; NSM 73.366.2

Construction

The nine-patch blocks are assembled in a set called sash or window-sash, made of yellow bars and red corner blocks. These colours are brighter because the cloth was new, while the pattern blocks were made from scraps of faded clothing.

Pieced quilt

Triple nine-patch

*made about 1900,
by Ada Maria Walfield,
Mosher's Island, Lunenburg County*

cotton
151 x 202 cm (59½˝ x 79½˝)
NSM 72.191.5

Construction

At the centre of each pattern block is a nine-patch, surrounded by another nine-patch, then another.

Neighbouring blocks are joined in a window-sash set. Small red squares brighten and unify the design, forming diagonal lines to connect the larger squares. The quilting follows both sides of each seam.

History

Ada Maria Walfield (1879-1983) referred to this as a patchwork quilt, a term especially appropriate for quilts made of mixed fabric scraps, or patches.

She made three quilts illustrated here (Q 10, 19, 30). In 1901 she married John Mosher, a fisherman. She said that she made all her quilts before her marriage– "after that I didn't have time!"

*Tinted photograph,
1895; private collection*

*LaHave Islands, Lunenburg County, about 1915.
Postcard; NSM 92.33.60*

Pieced quilt

Rob Peter to pay Paul

made in the late 1800s,
probably Kings County

wool top; cotton back and filler
190 x 204 cm (75˝x 80¼˝)
NSM 71.146.2

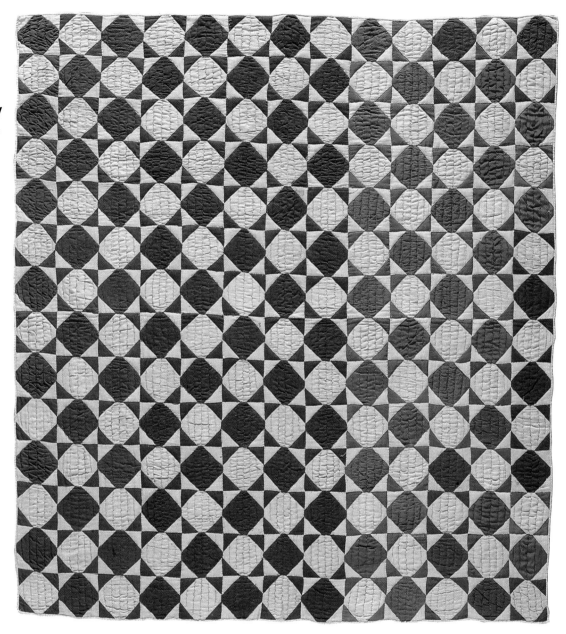

Construction

In 'rob Peter to pay Paul' quilt patterns, what is dark in one block is light in the next. There is no set to separate the blocks, so other designs emerge.

With colours reversed in alternating blocks, light and dark stars appear all over the quilt. The diagonal lines seem to be curved because the shape in the centre of each block is not pointed, so your eye moves back and forth to connect straight lines.

Pieced quilt

Windmill

*made about 1935,
by Mrs Vincent Dunlop,
Shelburne*

*cotton
177 x 189 cm (69¾″ x 74¼″)
NSM 72.82*

Construction

This quilt and the next, drawn on graph paper, are identical before adding colour. Each consists of two alternating pattern blocks–a nine-patch and an octagon (a square with corners replaced by dark triangles). For both quilts, the octagon block remains the same.

In the blue quilt, the nine-patch is shaded to form a dark X; in the red quilt, the X remains white. Two very different patterns are produced with this single alteration.

In the red quilt, the blocks have been tipped on the diagonal.

Pieced quilt

Snowball

made about 1890,
by Abbie P. (Locke) Spinney,
Melvern Square,
Annapolis County

cotton
172 x 194 cm (67¾″ x 76½″)
NSM 70.59.3

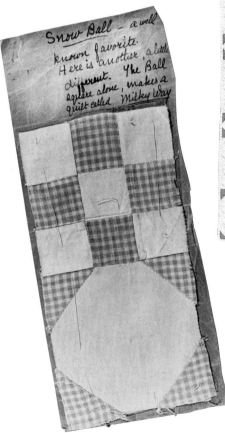

Sample pattern block, Yarmouth
County, early 1900s; NSM 73.30.22

Newspaper clipping, The Maritime
Farmer, *Saint John, N.B., 1920s;*
NSM

Pieced quilt

Flying geese

made in 1893, by Marie (Blinn) Thibodeau, Church Point, Digby County

cotton
150 x 200 cm
(59˝ x 78¾˝)
NSM 72.104

History
Marie Thibodeau made this quilt as a gift for her daughter Margaret when she married Michael Walsh.

Pieced quilt

Pinwheel

*made about 1885,
probably Baddeck,
Victoria County*

*cotton
164 x 188 cm
(64½″ x 74″)
NSM 72.349.1*

Construction
Rows of small triangles add complexity
to the basic pinwheel design.

Q 16

Pieced quilt

Sawtooth diamond

*made about 1882,
Saulnierville, Digby County*

*cotton
160 x 183 cm (63″ x 72″)
NSM 85.33.2*

Construction

Polka dot fabrics in this quilt offer an interesting variation on the traditional use of red and white.

History

Although it is difficult to generalize about regional or cultural differences, Acadians in some regions favoured a large, single design motif and bold colour. This quilt is said to have been made for a wedding.

Sawtooth diamond, made in 1901, by Margaret (Thibodeau) Walsh, Yarmouth 80 x 98 cm (31½″ x 38½″) NSM 77.13.4

This quilt was made for the birth of the maker's daughter. Margaret Walsh's mother made the flying geese quilt (Q 14).

Pieced quilt

Crossed squares

made about 1920,
probably Middleton,
Annapolis County

cotton
210 x 210 cm
(82½˝ x 82½˝)
NSM 79.61.1

Construction

This unusually large pattern block (70 cm, 27½˝) displays an excellent sampling of shirting and dress fabrics.

Unlike most quilts in the collection, this is pieced entirely by machine.

Simpson's catalogue for spring &
summer 1923

Pieced quilt

Star block, herringbone set

made about 1850, perhaps by a Mrs Douglas, LaHave Islands, Lunenburg County

cotton; old quilt filler; linen back
177 x 216 cm (69¾" x 85")
NSM 72.191.1

Construction

The fabric in the set is chintz, which still retains its original glazing. Rather than a wool or cotton batt, the filler is an older, worn quilt. The pattern block of this interior quilt is an eight-pointed star made of diamonds, alternating with a plain set block.

History

It is said that Mrs Douglas died in 1865. This quilt was found later in an abandoned house by Ada Walfield (see Q 10).

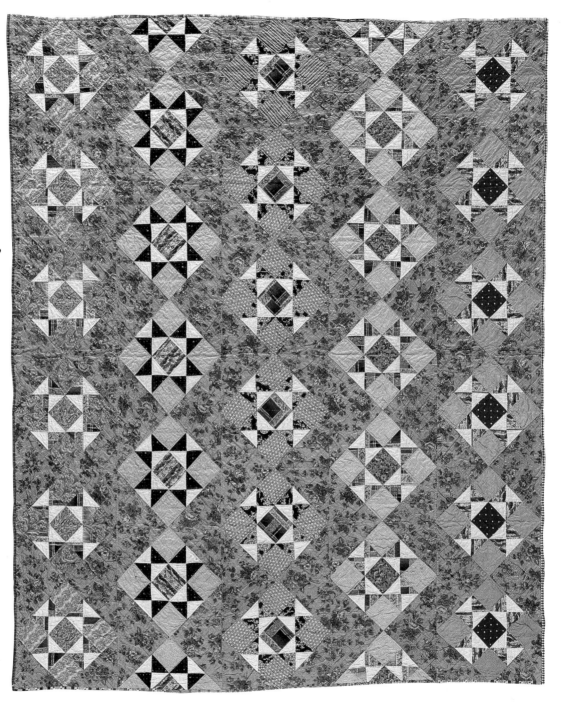

Pieced quilt

Pinwheel, herringbone set

*made about 1900,
by Ada Maria Walfield,
Mosher's Island,
Lunenburg County*

*cotton; old quilt filler
175 x 200 cm (69˝ x 78¾˝)
NSM 72.191.2*

Construction

The maker borrowed the idea for the set from an older quilt (Q 18), replacing the star block with a simple pinwheel. Like the older quilt, this too has a worn quilt filler; its pattern is an eight-pointed star in herringbone set, almost identical to Q 18.

The set is made with matching fabric, purchased new. The pieced blocks also include six colourways of another fabric design, bought as new remnants—the stamped bolt numbers still show.

Q 20

Pieced quilt

T-star

made about 1890,
Windsor,
Hants County

cotton
192 x 194 cm
(75½˝ x 76½˝)
NSM 73.366.1

Construction

This block is based on a nine-patch grid. The pattern block is nearly the same as the star in Q 18, but four bars are added in the corners. Each bar is the stem of a capital T.

Pieced quilt

Cat's paw or bear's paw

made about 1900, by Sussanah Mosher, Mosher's Island, Lunenburg County

cotton
163 x 186 cm (64″ x 73¼″)
NSM 72.191.4

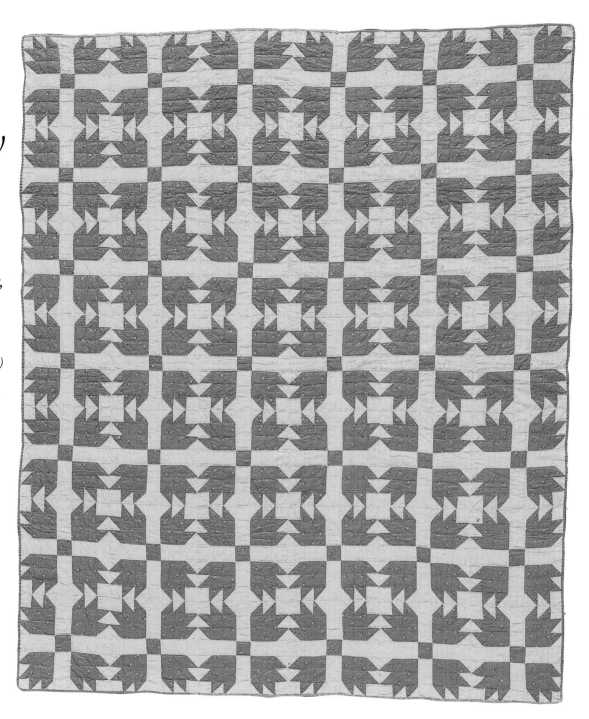

Construction

This pattern is more often seen set with squares or strips (see Chapter 4, Patterns for Sets). Without a set to separate them, the pattern blocks connect, making the basic unit more difficult to recognize.

History

Sussanah Mosher was the mother-in-law of Ada (Walfield) Mosher (see Q 10).

Pieced quilt

Fisherman's reel

*made about 1930s,
signed "M.F." in quilting,
probably Shelburne County*

cotton
171 x 189 cm (67¼˝ x 74¼˝)
NSM 91.73.1

Construction

This pattern is also known as 'double X' or 'fox and geese'. The shapes appear to float because the bars of the sash set are white, matching the background of the pattern blocks.

66

Pieced quilt

Maple-leaf

with signatures

*made about 1952,
by the United Baptist
Ladies Aid,
Port Greville,
Cumberland County*

*cotton
165 x 184 cm (65˝x 72½˝)
NSM 91.123*

appliqué

History

This quilt, like many others, was acquired without a history. With family names as the clue, it was possible to discover where it was made and to locate one of the makers. She said that the names are those of the women who worked on the quilt, and that it was sold to raise money for their church.

For other fundraising quilts, people in a community often paid to have their names embroidered.

Pieced quilt

Schoolhouse

*made about 1915,
by Deana (Hirtle) Dauphinee,
Bridgewater, Lunenburg County*

*cotton; 158 x 207 cm (62¼˝x 81½˝)
NSM 75.109.6*

History

Deana Dauphinee (c1835–c1928) made this quilt for her granddaughter, Marion, who later became principal of the Halifax Ladies' College, from 1940 to 1973. 'Marion' is embroidered in one corner. The schoolhouse motif became popular for quilts in the late 1800s.

In the United States, Artemus Ward wrote in 1862 of "a sea of upturned faces in the red schoolhouse". This image became a symbol of the American free public school system.

Most old wooden schools in Nova Scotia, however, were painted white not red.

Pieced quilt

Star of Bethlehem

dated 1925,
Mahone Bay,
Lunenburg County

cotton
190 x 190 cm (75″x 75″)
NSM 73.137.5

Construction

Each star is made of eight diamond-shaped points; as well, each point is made up of nine smaller diamond-shaped pieces.

History

Eight-pointed stars were popular in Lunenburg County quilts; more often they were made with triangles (see Q 18).

On one corner is written "1925 – Star of Bethlehem", but unfortunately the maker did not include her name.

Pieced quilt

Tumbling blocks

*made about 1890,
by Abbie (Locke)
Spinney,
Melvern Square,
Annapolis County*

*cotton
184 x 195 cm
(72½˝ x 76¾˝)
NSM 70.59.5*

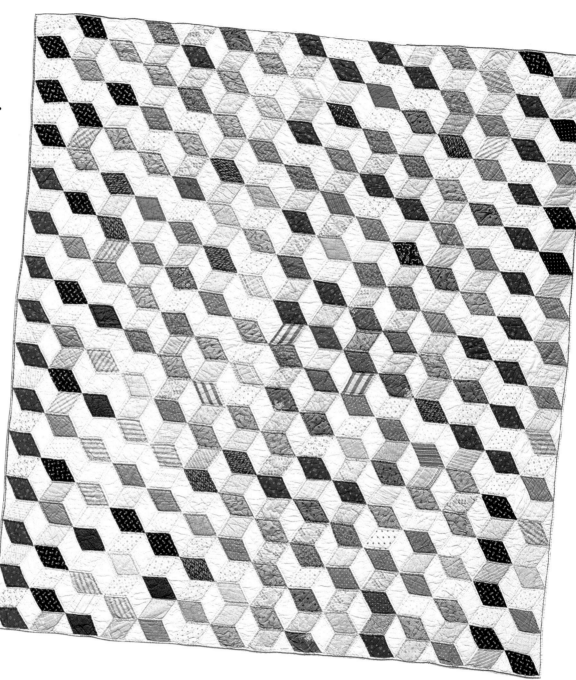

Construction

This optical illusion is created with a single diamond shape (see also Q 35). Careful placement of light, medium and dark fabrics gives a three-dimensional effect.

History

Abbie Spinney (1820–1910) also made quilt Q 13.

Pieced quilt

Broken star

made about 1940,
Nova Scotia

cotton
240 x 242 cm (94½˝ x 95½˝)
NSM Z842

Construction

Made from a popular commercial pattern, this quilt was based on a traditional star of diamond pieces. Careful placement of bright colours adds to the energy of the design.

The quilting is on the seam ('in the ditch' as quilters now say) rather than beside it; designs follow the published pattern.

Pieced quilt

Broken star

made about 1939,
by Margaret
MacInnis Young,
Western Shore,
Lunenburg County

cotton
218 x 226 cm (85¾˝ x 89˝)
NSM 68.124

Construction

This quilt is made in the same pattern as the previous one, but with softer colours and prints the effect is very different. The quilting is simpler and less ornate. In this example, the circle of white squares in the background, which breaks the star-burst, is less conspicuous than in the previous quilt with its stronger colours.

History

This quilt was made as a wedding present.

Q 29

Pieced quilt top

Military quilt

made about 1870,
by Corporal Thomas Noonan,
Melville Island, Halifax

wool; no filler or back
215 x 230 cm (84½˝ x 90½˝)
NSM 79.84.1

Thomas Noonan,
right, late 1860s.
Photo by W.D.
O'Donnell;
NSM 79.84.2

History

Quilts made from soldiers' uniforms have been recorded in Britain, Canada, and the United States. Thomas Noonan served in the British Army during the Crimean War (1854–1856), and later worked as warden at the military prison near Halifax.

Corporal Noonan never completed his quilt. He died on 1 February 1874, aged 38, as a result of exposure after rescuing a boy who had fallen through the ice of the North-West Arm.

Construction

Because of the thickness of the uniform cloth and the size of the pieces, it must have been a challenge to sew this top. As a result, the pattern became less precise further from the centre. Most of the shapes are diamonds, but small hexagons also occur at the centres of the stars.

Thomas Walker, a Crimean War veteran,
in hospital at Chelsea, England, painted by
Thomas W. Wood, 1856; courtesy of the
Royal College of Surgeons of England, London

Walker was wounded at Inkerman, as the sign above his head indicates. Corporal Noonan received medals for service in battles at Alma, Balaclava, Sebastopol, and Inkerman.

Red was the primary uniform colour of the British army; however, blue, black, green, cream, and yellow were also used for details such as cuffs and collars.

Pieced quilt

Tulip

made about 1900,
by Ada Maria Walfield,
Mosher's Island,
Lunenburg County

cotton
148 x 184 cm (58¼˝ x 72½˝)
NSM 72.48.4

Construction

Because there is no sash or set, it is difficult to pick out the pattern block— three pieced flowers on a branching stem. This quilt includes quite a bit of machine sewing, used for piecing and even for the appliqué stems.

With no filler, this is what some people call a summer quilt.

73

Log cabin quilt top

Light and dark diamonds

made about 1890,
Yarmouth

wool on cotton; no filler or back
186 x 219 cm (73¼″ x 86¼″)
NSM 73.80.3

Construction

Made with woolen fabrics, this quilt was never backed and finished. The block is rather small, approximately 18 cm (7″).

This popular shading of the basic block allows many arrangements. Here are three common ones using the same number of blocks, placed differently:

Log Cabin Quilts

Log cabin quilts are built up by sewing strips of fabric to a foundation cloth. To make a block, work begins with a centre square. Each log is sewn to cover the outer edge of the previous one. Light and dark fabrics produce effects of sunshine and shadow. Various patterns can be created by arranging the blocks.

Many log cabin quilts were never quilted; some were tied.

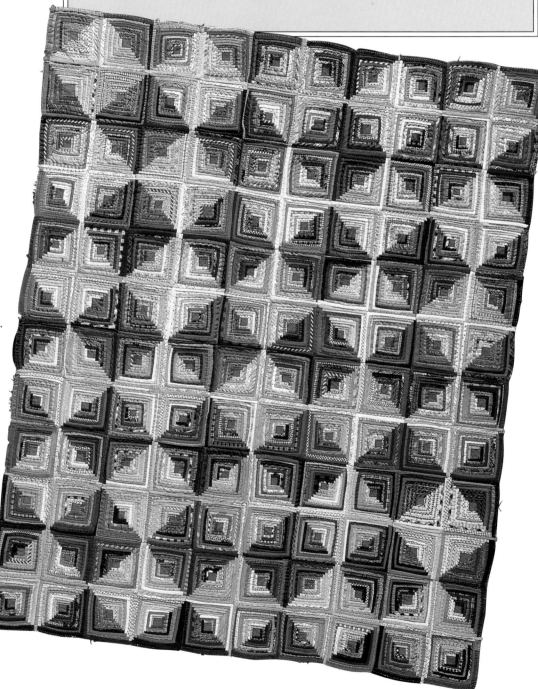

Log cabin quilt

Courthouse steps

*made about 1885,
probably Halifax*

*silk, velvet; no filler; cotton back
172 x 174 cm (67¾″ x 68½″)
NSM 69.3.5*

Construction

The back is made of blue sateen. With no quilting, the layers are connected by embroidery stitches showing a repeating wing-shaped motif on the quilt back.

This shading of the block allows only two main patterns.

History

Several of these logs were lacrosse tournament ribbons, dated 1871 to 1880. Sometimes, an entire quilt was made of silk award ribbons or cigar bands. Cigars were sold in bunches tied together with silk ribbons.

*Unfinished cushion top, made about 1890, probably Pictou County
65 x 65 cm (25½″ x 25½″)
silk on cotton; NSM 74.95.1*

These cigar bands are sewn onto a foundation cloth, similar to log-cabin construction.

Q 33

Log cabin quilt

Pineapple or windmill blades

made about 1900, by Susan Mutart (Allen) Larder, Stewiacke, Colchester County

cotton; no filler
204 x 212 cm (80¼˝ x 83½˝)
NSM 88.74.19

The Larder home, Stewiacke, about 1905; private collection

Susan Mutart (Allen) Larder (1861-1956). Photo by D.R. Pridham, Amherst, 1890s; private collection

Construction

Instead of the usual placement of logs on four sides of each block, there are more logs laid across the corners. The basic block is very large—50 cm (20˝) —so only sixteen are needed to make the whole top.

Silk Quilts and Crazy Quilts

In the mid-1800s, many fine dress silks were available in a wide range of colours and textures. People traded remnants. As well, women's magazines advertised packets of silk scraps from dress factories.

Crazy quilts, made of velvets and silks with plenty of embroidery, were very fashionable in the late 1800s. Most often, they were intended for display on parlour sofas rather than as bedcovers. Although crazy quilts do not usually have a filler, people tend to call them quilts because the tops are assembled from many pieces.

The word 'crazy' refers to something erratic. It is also used to describe ceramics with crazed or cracked glaze.

Godey's Lady's Book,
Philadelphia, March 1859

Pieced quilt

Multiple nine-patch

dated 1862,
marked "L.B.A.",
probably Amherst,
Cumberland County

silk; cotton filler and back
164 x 215 cm (64½″ x 84½″)
NSM 72.187.2

Construction

The quilt top is laid out like a large nine-patch, with several smaller nine-patch portions.

The quilting design bears little connection with the pattern of the top. Because of this, and because of the difficulty of using black thread on the black silk, this example may have been quilted from the back.

History

This quilt was discovered as a filler inside another one; the fragile silk had been patched several times before being covered up. Although dark colours were used in clothing of the period, it is unusual to see such a sombre bedcover, evoking a feeling of sadness and mystery. L.B.A. might have been the maker or the owner, or perhaps this quilt commemorated the death of a loved one.

Q 35

Pieced quilt

Box illusion

made about 1850,
Bridgewater or Halifax

silk, velvet; cotton back
91 x 140 cm (36˝ x 55¼˝)
NSM 69.140.119

Construction

Using the same pattern as quilt Q 26, a very different effect is created with silk and velvet. These fabrics probably came from waistcoats and cravats as well as dresses.

Because the backing fabric (printed cotton, perhaps from the 1830s) was not exposed to much light, it is in excellent condition. The museum also owns a piece of identical print that has lost much of its original colour, especially the greens and yellows.

In doing patchwork, care must be taken to cut all your papers of the exact size; after which baste your silk (or whatever material you are using) over the papers; and when you have a quantity so covered, choose your colours to harmonize; after which, connect the edges by sewing very closely and even, leaving the papers in until the whole is put together; after which, undo the basting-stitches, pick out the papers, line the work with glazed calico, and quilt it in any pattern you please, so as to keep the lining and cover tight together; or it may be knotted in the centre of each star, with any bright-coloured floss-silk or Berlin wool.

Godey's Lady's Book, Philadelphia, September 1854

Q 36

Lillian Eagles with members of her family. Courtesy of Douglas Eagles

Crazy quilt

made about 1885, by Lillian Maybelle (Lockhart) Eagles, Kentville, Kings County

silk, velvet; cotton back and ruffled edge
182 x 207 cm (71½˝ x 81½˝)
NSM 73.7

Construction

To ornament the velvet, silk, and cotton pieces, many different embroidery stitches and motifs were employed– a spider's web, a woman, a man with a pig. There are also a few flowers painted on the fabric.

Perhaps more than one person stitched these decorations. Some are quite sophisticated, others are much simpler.

History

"Grandma [Eagles] made many quilts.... She always seemed to have a quilt in the frames and when any-one came in she got them to put in a stitch or two." Lillian Eagles lived from 1866 to 1962.

Caulfeild & Saward, 1887 edition

Q 37

Crazy quilt

made about 1888,
by Christianna (McDonald) Henry,
Halifax

silk, velvet; cotton filler; silk back
147 x 190 cm (58″ x 75″)
NSM 71.92

Construction

Spider-webs and Japanese fan motifs appeared on many crazy quilts. In this example, embroidery was also used to enhance the fancy brocaded fabrics.

History

Christianna McDonald (born Antigonish 1823, died Halifax 1900), was married to the Hon. William Alexander Henry, a father of Confederation and later a judge of the Supreme Court. The quilt may have been made for her son, Hugh; his initials "H McD H" are embroidered on one piece. About the same time, Mrs Henry also made a similar crazy quilt with a blue border, and sent it to a relative in England.

Christianna Henry (left), with her daughter, 1860s. Ambrotype photo; NSM 92.51.15

The stitched letters and dates "VR 1838/88" likely refer to Victoria Regina. Victoria became queen in 1837, but was not crowned until 1838. Her Golden (50th) Jubilee was celebrated in 1887.

If Cristianna Henry did not finish the quilt until 1888, the inscription may refer to the 50th anniversary of the coronation instead.

Henry House, Barrington Street, Halifax. Photo by A.W. Wallace, 1924; NSM 76.116.158

Crazy quilt

*dated 1885,
signed "HLT",
probably Wolfville,
Kings County*

*silk, velvet; factory quilted silk
back; cotton lace edge
164 x 166 cm (64½″ x 65¼″)
NSM 80.1*

*Caulfeild & Saward,
1887 edition*

Construction

Fine dress silks are attached to a backing
with a wide variety of embroidery stitches.
The strawberry motifs in two corners use
chenille thread for a raised appearance.
'Chenille', French for caterpillar, describes
the fuzzy appearance of the thread.

History

This is the finest example of a Victorian
crazy quilt yet discovered in Nova Scotia.
In spite of much research trying to identify
HLT, the maker remains a mystery.

The lace edge suggests that this crazy
quilt may have been made as a table cover.

Boy and woman with a wholecloth quilt, Guysborough County, about 1900. Photo by W.H. Buckley; PANS

Wholecloth Quilts

The top of a wholecloth quilt is made with only one fabric, plain or printed. White quilts are the most familiar in this classification and were often made for special occasions, such as weddings. With designs created only by quilting stitches and the shadows cast on the surface, white quilts demonstrate the skill of a fine quilter.

None of these quilts is 'stuffed'; any raised effect is produced only through the use of quilting stitches spaced closely or far apart.

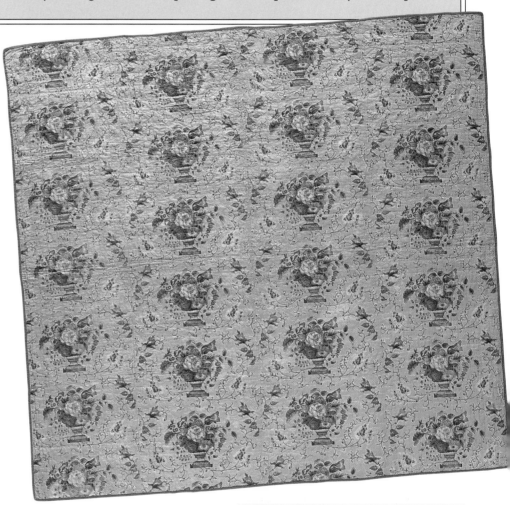

Q 39

Wholecloth quilt

made about 1840,
by Mary E. (Irish) Symonds,
Falmouth, Hants County

cotton
228 x 256 cm (89¾˝ x 100¾˝)
NSM 65.215.24

Construction

The printed fabric may date from about 1830. It is said that this quilt was made from four-poster bed hangings. It may also have been part of a matching set of curtains and bedcover. Although decorative, the quilt would have been made relatively quickly and easily; the quilting pattern consists only of widely spaced crossed lines that form squares, approximately 5 cm (2˝).

History

Mary Symonds (1775–1867) and four succeeding generations of her family used this quilt.

"View from Retreat Farm, Windsor, N.S.", near Falmouth, late 1830s. Lithograph (detail) by William Eagar; NSM 80.63.12

Q 40

Wholecloth quilt

*made about 1890,
by Adeline Crossman,
Debert, Colchester
County*

*cotton
165 x 214 cm (65″x 84¼″)
NSM 75.35.1*

History

Later remarried, Adeline Crossman Rector died in 1930.

Construction

Against the intense red fabric, shadows from slanting light are needed to show up the quilted design. Use of coloured fabric in Nova Scotian wholecloth quilts is unusual. Quilted with red thread, the designs are arranged in a medallion or framed format.

Q 41

Wholecloth quilt

made about 1850, in the Foster family, Torbrook, Annapolis County

cotton; wool filler
204 x 211 cm
(80¼˝ x 83˝)
NSM 73.145.2

History

It is uncertain whether this quilt was made by Mrs Ezekiel Foster or by her daughter-in-law, Susan Foster (born 1827).

Construction

The pineapple, symbol of hospitality, was a popular motif in the late 1700s and early 1800s.

Made visible with a slanting light, ripples in the wool filler seem to indicate the use of a machine-carded batt, about 30 cm (12˝) wide.

Wholecloth quilt

made in 1897, by Margaret Ann (Magee) Spurr, Torbrook, Annapolis County

cotton
204 x 212 cm
(80¼˝ x 83½˝)
NSM 82.53

Construction

As in many quilts, large pieces of fabric for this top were seamed by machine. Also, the binding was sewn by machine to the front, then turned to the back and finished by hand.

History

This quilt is inscribed "M. Spurr/1897" in ink. Margaret Ann Magee (1854–1924) married George Edward Spurr in 1876. According to a descendant, the couple met at the cemetery while Mr Spurr was visiting his first wife's grave.

Margaret Spurr and family, about 1895. Private collection

Wholecloth quilt

White quilt, with valance

*made 1850–1855,
by Lavinia Jane Outhit,
Margaretsville,
Annapolis County*

*cotton; wool filler
248 x 252 cm (97½″ x 99¼″)
+ valance
61 x 639 cm (24″ x 251½″)
NSM 84.35A-B*

Construction

The quilted valance is a unique example in the province. As well, the fine and intricate quilting combined with large size make this quilt and valance a remarkable pair. As the valance has never been washed, pencil lines to mark out the quilting are still visible. The motifs are thrown into relief by the parallel lines of background ('crêpe') quilting, 0.8 cm (¼″) apart. The central motif, a 16-pointed star, is framed by borders of wreaths and vines.

The edges are finished with a running stitch on a tape binding. This method was far more common in Britain than in Nova Scotia.

History

It is said that Lavinia Jane Outhit (1828-1914) made this quilt for her marriage to Thomas A. Margeson in 1855.

Q *44*

Wholecloth quilt

Infant's silk quilt made about 1850, attributed to Amelia (Haliburton) Gilpin, possibly Hants County

silk; wool filler
95 x 108 cm (37½" x 42½")
NSM 65.217.1

Construction

The quilting motifs resemble those from Wales and the west of England. The quilt edge was finished with a running stitch sewn through a ribbon binding, which is more common on old British quilts.

A two-ply silk thread was used for quilting.

"The Residence of Judge Haliburton", Windsor, N.S., c 1840. Drawn by W.H. Bartlett; NSM 65.206.308

History

There is some uncertainty as to the date and the Nova Scotian origin of this quilt. It has been attributed to Amelia Gilpin (whose first child was born in 1850). However, the design motifs and material suggest that it could be older and not locally made. Instead, it might have come through family connections in Britain.

Amelia Gilpin was a daughter of Thomas C. Haliburton, politician, judge, and writer. He is best known for his fictional character Sam Slick.

Appliqué

When one piece of cloth is applied on top of another, the construction is called appliqué. The technique was used to ornament clothing as well as quilt tops. Appliqué permits curving shapes, whereas most pieced construction uses shapes made with straight lines.

Appliqué quilts, using new materials and intricate patterns, were often the special quilts in a household.

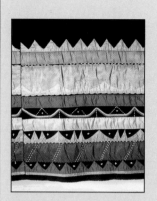

Ribbon appliqué, with beads, on a Mi'kmaq skirt, made by Mary Morris Thomas, about 1845. NSM 10.7

Catherine Maloney, Shubenacadie, 1905. NSM 13.15 a

Appliqué and pieced quilt

Sawtooth with vine

made about 1900, probably MacKenzie family, Scotsburn, Pictou County

cotton
180 x 180 cm (71″ x 71″)
NSM 92.84.2

Construction

This quilt combines two construction methods—the straight lines of the sawtooth edges are pieced, while the curving lines of the vine and flowers are appliqué.

Appliqué quilt

Royal portraits

made about 1902, attributed to Addie Wolfe, Conquerall Bank, Lunenburg County

cotton; silk floss
181 x 220 cm
(71½˝ x 86½˝)
NSM 74.138

Construction

The frames for the portraits were pieced by machine with strips of red, white, and blue; these were then applied to the quilt top by machine. The rest of the quilt was hand-stitched. The commercial souvenir portraits were derived from photographs; these were printed by a half-tone printing press, not in a photographer's darkroom.

History

The thistle, shamrock, and rose in the border symbolize Scotland, Ireland, and England. The portraits depict King Edward VII and Queen Alexandra, Queen Victoria, and the Prince and Princess of Wales (later George V and Queen Mary).

Victoria died in 1901, so she is edged in black, for mourning. Her eldest son, Edward VII, wears the robes of his coronation in August 1902.

The first prize label from 1902 reads "Quilt, Patchwork, calico", which does not seem to describe this bedcover accurately. Perhaps the label belonged with another quilt made by Addie Wolfe.

Appliqué quilt

Tulip

*made about 1930,
possibly Halifax*

*cotton
176 x 213 cm
(69¼˝ x 83¾˝)
NSM 78.28.2*

Construction

Although this quilt has faded from washing
and use, its pastel colours and style of
appliqué are typical of the period from the
1920s to the 1940s.

Appliqué quilt

Snowflake

made about 1870,
by Margaret Roy,
Westville, Pictou County

cotton
178 x 216 cm (70″x 85″)
NSM 77.19.2

Construction

The central motif looks as if one large piece of red cloth had been folded and cut like a paper snowflake. In fact, each point is a separate piece. The border is also made up of smaller units. Without a separate binding, the front edge is turned to the back and finished.

The lines of quilting do not relate to the snowflake design.

History

Margaret Roy came from Glasgow, Scotland, about 1854, to be with her son, John. He became manager of the Black Diamond Coal Mine in Westville.

Appliqué quilt

Oak leaf and acorn

made about 1850,
probably Clementsport,
Annapolis County

cotton
206 x 240 cm (81˝ x 94½˝)
NSM 76.97

Construction

Oak leaf and acorn designs, and the use of red and green, were very popular in the mid-1800s. Before 1875, green was commonly made by using blue and yellow dyes. The more permanent blue remained after the yellow faded.

This quilt was entirely hand-pieced and seamed. Although they appear to have been assembled in square blocks, the appliqué motifs were sewn onto strips. Crossing diagonal lines of quilting were scaled to fit the design, and pass through it at critical points such as the leaf tips.

Appliqué quilt

Rose

made about 1850,
by Sadie Warne,
New Tusket,
Digby County

cotton
225 x 227 cm
(88½″x 89¼″)
NSM 78.69

Sadie Warne (right) with her sister Cynthia and their mother. Ambrotype photo; private collection

Construction

This is an outstanding example of appliqué from the mid-1800s, in a typical format of nine large pattern blocks, approximately 59 cm (23″), surrounded by a vine border.

All of the seams were sewn by hand, as was the binding to front and back. Thrift is demonstrated in the backing fabric, made with 15 pieces. In the flowers, the quilted lines align with the design, while in the leaves they imitate veins. The remainder is quilted with diagonal lines, crossing approximately 2 cm (¾″) apart.

Leaves and stems which now appear blue would have been dark green.

History

According to family stories, Sadie Warne (1826–1886) was fondly regarded by those who knew her. She lived with her younger married sister, Cynthia Sabean, and helped to take care of her children.

93

CHAPTER 6

Other Quilt Types
Not Represented in the Museum Collection

*A*s previously stated, the exhibition *Old Nova Scotian Quilts* was organized according to quilt types. However there are gaps in the museum collection. The quilts included here are Nova Scotian but are not owned by the museum.

Framed/ Medallion Quilts

One regrettable gap in the collection is the 'framed' or 'medallion' quilt. This quilt top from the Annapolis Valley is pieced with fine fabrics from the late 1700s. It is not known whether it was made in Nova Scotia or brought here from England. There is a strong British influence in its construction and overall design, but this would be expected in a quilt top made in Nova Scotia or in New England during this period. Paper templates would have been used to piece the combination of geometric shapes (diamonds, hexagons, truncated diamonds, and equilateral triangles). Such a quilt, with its central motif and framing, required that the maker have the financial resources to buy enough fabric to complete an overall design, unlike the many pieced quilts built up block by block.

Pieced quilt top, roller-printed and block-printed cottons, early 1800s. Private collection

Figurative Quilts

Another quilt type not represented in the collection is the 'figurative', 'story', or 'picture' quilt. Without more research, it would be difficult to assert that they were rarely made; however, surviving examples are uncommon.

Fortunately, three examples done by a woman in the 1930s and 1940s in Lunenburg County were valued and preserved by family members.

Sarah (Frank) Robar was born in Upper Cornwall, Lunenburg County, in 1871. According to the family, 'Aunt Sarah' lived a hard-scrabble existence with a difficult husband, bringing up eight children. In spite of the bleakness and poverty in her life, she managed to find a creative outlet through writing poetry and making appliqué picture blocks that she often gave to friends and family. Many came to be used as potholders. Fortunately some blocks were assembled into quilt tops. Sarah Robar drew inspiration for her pictures from several sources: local scenes and family events, such as her grand-niece and nephews bringing in a Christmas tree; images based on stories and poems (such as "The Burial of Sir Thomas More") that she recalled from school readers; and scenes from magazines. Her spiritual faith was also expressed through picture blocks.

Blocks in two of the quilt tops were made in the 1930s and many of the same fabrics turn up on both surfaces. Sarah Robar depended on the generosity of family and friends to provide her with fabric scraps. Her grand-niece, Jean Jess, recalls Aunt Sarah visiting and picking cloth from the scrap basket to create her blocks. Sarah's gratitude is expressed through a poem titled "My Friends":

Sarah Robar spinning; NSM

> *Who says my friends are false to me*
> *who says that they are not true*
> *if it was not for my loving friends*
> *what would this shut in do…*
>
> *Goods for a quilt they send to me*
> *from every home around*
> *for me to work and pass the hours*
> *a goodly store abound…*
>
> Poem pencilled in a scribbler, 1930s

Block from picture quilt made by Sarah Robar, 1930s; courtesy of Jean Jess

A third quilt top was made by Sarah in the 1940s, and it is markedly different in feeling from the other two. Wartime images in sombre colours reflect the anxiety of the times. Sarah was aging and in deteriorating health, so the stitching is more crudely executed. She died in 1950. This quilt is now on loan to the Parkdale-Maplewood Museum in Lunenburg County.

Picture quilt made by Sarah Robar,
1940s; private collection

The strong American tradition of figurative quilts with patriotic, political, and social themes is not in evidence in the province. Historically, Nova Scotians have not tended to give public expression to their sentiments and viewpoints, so the dearth of this particular type of quilt is not unexpected. References to such quilts do not turn up in written records until the 1940s. The following excerpt from a W.I. newsletter gives an indication of a developing trend toward thematic renderings on quilts.

> *The display of appliqued quilts featured many patterns and there were some patchwork quilts as well.... The members of the Upper Stewiacke group were really ambitious—their design was a map of the Dominion of Canada with the industries illustrated. The Nova Scotia industries were illustrated in more detail. A member of the Noel Institute displayed an embroidered quilt with designs depicting various phases of Canadian life.*
>
> *Home and Country*, January-February 1950

After the Second World War, Canadians began to consider more seriously the question of cultural identity, and this is reflected in such quilts. No longer wishing to be considered a colonial outpost of the British Empire, and yet not temperamentally suited to adopt an American-style nationalism, Canada moved through the 1940s, '50s and into the '60s trying to develop its own agenda and national themes. For example, in 1955, a quilt commemorating the 200th anniversary of the Expulsion of the Acadians was exhibited and won honourable mention at the Canadian National Exhibition, Toronto. Designed by Marguerite Gates and made by the Port Williams Women's Institute, Kings County, it reflected a growing desire to express cultural and historical themes intimately connected to the region.

While more recent quilts are not the subject of this book (the 'youngest' quilts included were made in the 1950s), it is perhaps worthwhile to project what future historians will see in the development of pictorial and thematic quilts in Nova Scotia after 1967, the centenary of Canadian confederation.

What will likely be observed is a trend for depiction of personal, family, and local histories and, through the 1980s and '90s, for presentation of themes concerned with social issues such as world peace, the environment, AIDS, and multiculturalism. Thematic quilts are almost always group projects initiated to raise consciousness or funds, and often both. The proliferation of such quilts will reveal that quiltmaking can always be relevant, not so much for the provision of essential bedding as for the opportunities to bring people closer together in friendship and understanding. These quilts are modern equivalents to the friendship and album quilts of an earlier time.

Centre section of the quilt designed by Marguerite Gates to commemorate the 200th anniversary of the Expulsion of the Acadians, 1955; NSM 65.214.34

Friendship and Album Quilts

In Nova Scotian quiltmaking, the terms 'friendship' and 'album' were sometimes interchangeable. Similar to the notion of an autograph album, autographed quilt blocks were collected by a woman from her friends, embroidered, and joined into a quilt top. At other times, several women would assemble their blocks to produce a gift for another. Pattern blocks could be made in a single predetermined design or all different, according to each maker's choice.

The Yarmouth County Museum owns an excellent example of a friendship quilt, made in 1881–82 by members of the Holy Trinity Church in Yarmouth. With drawings and inscriptions in indelible ink, this nine-patch with plain set blocks is a lively testimony to good-natured community feeling. The quilt helped to raise funds for mission work.

The nine-patch block (frame type) was a favourite for album and signature quilts as there was plenty of room to add names.

Friendship quilt, 1881–82; pieced nine-patch
block, with ink drawings and inscriptions.
Yarmouth County Museum

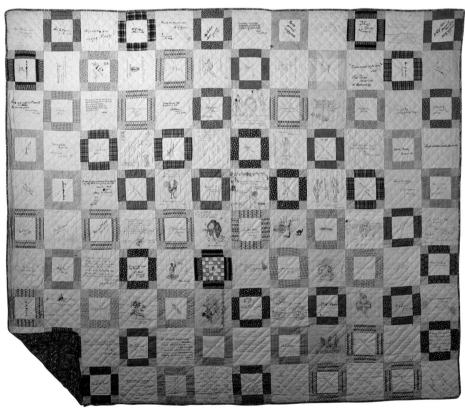

Quilted Clothing

Although this book is primarily about bed quilts, quilting was occasionally used in other contexts. Throughout human history and from distinctly different cultures, there have been examples of quilted clothing, as well as articles of clothing using patchwork and appliqué techniques. Although we know that quilted petticoats were high fashion in the 1700s and early 1800s, little written evidence has been found to indicate whether quilting in more everyday apparel was common. However, two Nova Scotian diarists have left a brief record.

After Margaret Michener (see Chapter 2, Diaries) remarried and left Hantsport for the United States, she continued her diary through several moves. In 1868, she was living in Delaware; on 9 January she wrote, "I quilted a skirt for Nettie [her daughter] out of a light shawl I had when I was a girl."

Twenty-five years later, on 12 April 1893, Mary Winton wrote in her diary, "I quilted a peticoat for Rosie" [her daughter]. Mary Winton and her husband kept the lighthouse on Gabarus Island, off the coast of Cape Breton, near Louisbourg. Her journal recorded the daily activities of carding, spinning, knitting, mat-making, quilting, and farming. In all likelihood, Rosie's petticoat would have been a practical piece of clothing, made for warmth rather than fashion.

The only other written reference to quilted clothing comes from another lighthouse keeper's family. Evelyn Richardson and her family lived on Bon Portage Island, off the southwest coast of Nova Scotia in Shelburne County. During the war years, she wrote:

> *From odd bits of inferior wool I quilt jackets for Morrill and the children to wear under their coats. The men's I make from khaki drill, the girls' from dress prints, and I quilt the different sections separately before putting the garment together. These garments take little wool and are warmer than sweaters—and far easier to make. I started making them before the present vogue for quilted jackets. My inspiration was an inner down jacket I saw advertised for sportswear, and I imitated this for Morrill to wear gunning. He liked his so well that all the other members of the family demanded one, too.*

Evelyn Richardson, *We Keep a Light*, 1945

It may be coincidental that two of the three references to quilted clothing came from lighthouse families; nevertheless, quilted clothing would have been very sensible for those facing the chilly winds of the Atlantic Ocean.

Less practical and more decorative is a jacket with log cabin construction made by Aminella Wentzell for her brother, Thomas Spidell. He would have cut quite a figure while walking in rural Lunenburg County. It is more likely that he wore it at home as a lounging jacket.

Pieced jacket, made about 1900 by Aminella Wentzell (1881-1977), Barss Corner, Lunenburg County. Parkdale-Maplewood Museum

Other Types Not Found in Nova Scotia

There are quilt types that have not been found in the province, such as 'broderie perse' (a form of appliqué using printed motifs cut from imported chintz), and a type of wholecloth quilt made of glazed woolen fabric. Although no examples exist, there is written evidence to indicate that 'palampores' (chintz bedcovers imported from India) were here, both in the early French settlement of Louisbourg (see Chapter 2, endnote 1) and also later, at least into the early 1800s.

Caspar Wollenhaupt was a shopkeeper in the town of Lunenburg with a large inventory of goods and fabrics; these were well itemized after his death in 1809. Our attention is drawn to two entries:

> No. 186   *21 Pieces Selampores*
>   *@ 20/P piece*   £ *21 / 0 / 0*
>
> No. 187   *9 ¾ yds Selampores*
>   *@ 1/*   */ 9 / 9*

The word 'selampore' appears nowhere in dictionaries of textile terms; because of the way in which S and P were sometimes written in older script, it is plausible that the inventory taker, unfamiliar with the word, may have spelled it incorrectly.

In the old British money system, there were 20 shillings to the pound. The items in the first entry are considerably more expensive (20 shillings or one pound per 'piece') than the second entry item (one shilling per yard), which leads us to suspect that the 'pieces' were fully made up, quilted palampores, whereas the second listing was yardage, to be made up into a quilt or other furnishings after purchase.

"The Patchwork Quilt" by E.W. Perry; Harper's Weekly, *New York, 21 December 1872*

Early examples of rather special quilts may turn up in a provincial quilt inventory. The chances become slimmer as time goes on. For over 70 years, Nova Scotia has been a favourite hunting ground for antique dealers interested in early North American furnishings. Untold thousands of artifacts have found their way from Nova Scotia into the New England antique marketplace, and so we will never know what was once here.

However, the story of quilting in Nova Scotia has less to do with creation of elaborate or unusual quilts, and more to do with production of functional but often visually pleasing quilts by hardworking, practical women. It is a story of continuity, of tradition and remarkable output, where hands of many generations have worked together to provide comfort for family, friends, and strangers, both at home and abroad.

Quiltmaking Today

*T*he contemporary development of quilting and quilt study has grown in Nova Scotia, as in most other parts of Canada and the United States, as well as in Europe, Australia, and Japan. While it is not the purpose of this book or related exhibition to explore modern quilt-making, perhaps a few notes will serve to assist succeeding projects as they study the topic. Quilts made in Nova Scotia today are not simply the product of a continuous quilt-making tradition. In addition to the rural survival of local preferences, quilters across the province have been more likely to derive inspiration, as well as patterns and specific techniques, from American sources. The largest influence has certainly been the great number of magazines and 'how-to' books, as well as books on quilt history. For example, wide popularity of Amish quilts now means that their designs and colour preferences far exceed the boundaries of Amish communities.

American influence has been particularly strong in recent decades as many prominent quilters from the United States have visited Nova Scotia to teach contemporary approaches to quiltmaking: Jinny Beyer, Nancy Crowe, Judy Dales, Jo Diggs, Chris Wolf Edmonds, Beth Gutcheon, Nancy Halpern, Roberta Horton, Michael James, Jean Ray Laury, Terrie Mangat, and Doreen Speckman. Most of them were brought here as part of the activities of the provincial quilting association, Mayflower Handquilters, established in 1974, and now, twenty years later, with over 250 members around the province.

In recent years, some Nova Scotian quilters have also become recognized not only in the province but across Canada, as teachers and for their work exhibited in museums and galleries, and represented in publication–Marilyn Crawford, Ruth Edsall, Polly Greene, Valerie Hearder, Christopher King, Anne Comfort Morrell, Barbara Robson, Dora Velleman, and others. Several are also known internationally.

As this is the first book on the history of quiltmaking in Nova Scotia, there is considerable work remaining to be done. We have searched for the pieces and threads that make up the historical fabric of quilt history in the province. It is hoped that this will encourage more people to bring out their quilted treasures for examination by museum curators and quilt historians, so that more pieces of our history will be available for extensive study and reconsideration in the future.

Care and Cleaning

Quilts are subject to deterioration caused by many factors. Important or fragile quilts should be cleaned by textile conservation specialists only. These can be contacted through the Canadian Association of Professional Conservators[1], the Canadian Conservation Institute[2] (CCI), and local museums.

Vacuuming

Initial cleaning should be done using a vacuum cleaner, set for low suction. In some circumstances, this will remove enough dust and dry dirt to make further cleaning avoidable. Protect the surface of the quilt with a piece of plastic window screening, with edges bound to prevent catching the fabric. Vacuum both sides of the quilt.

Washing

The following remarks apply only to cotton or woolen quilts that have been washed previously without any differential shrinking of materials or running of dyes. Silk quilts or quilts made with a combination of materials are not included. For those, and for any important or fragile quilts, consult a textile conservator. Most quilts that cannot be washed can still be vacuumed.

Any damage must be repaired or protected before cleaning. Weak areas should be covered with polyester sheer curtain material, or similar; baste this to sound fabric around the deterioration.

Before proceeding, carefully examine both surfaces and all edges of the quilt. If you decide your quilt must be washed and is strong enough, we can make a few suggestions.

If you choose to proceed, test all colours for fastness. To each area to be tested, with an eyedropper apply a few drops of the water to be used (about 25° C to 30° C/ 75° to 85° F). Press blotting paper against the wetted area and check for colour transfer. If there is any transfer, do not continue. Test again with a solution of detergent in water if you intend to use that. CCI Note 13/9 (see Bibliography) deals with washing with anionic detergent.

The ideal method is to wash a quilt in a flat position, without folds; conservators use a special washing table. In a household situation, some people recommend washing a quilt by hand in a bathtub. The major difficulties with this method are that the quilt must be washed with many folds, and that it must be lifted from the tub while still wet and therefore very heavy. Great strain can be caused to a quilt in this situation.

Never wash a quilt in an automatic washing machine. However, we have discovered that a washing machine can be a useful tool if it is not used in the regular way. We suggest using the machine only as a tub and as a water extractor. A great advantage to this method is that the quilt is not picked up while it is at its heaviest. Also, most of the water is extracted quickly, thereby limiting potential movement of colours.

Fill the tub with lukewarm water. Gently lower the quilt into the water. Allow the cloth and batt to absorb the water naturally and swell before you continue. When the quilt has relaxed in the water, gently move water through the quilt by hand only. Never use the agitation or wash cycle of the machine. Do not squeeze, twist, wring, or otherwise strain the material.

Do not remove the quilt from the tub. When you are ready to rinse, drain the water. Ensure that the quilt is distributed evenly, without any strain. With the machine lid open, activate the spin cycle by hand. In order to make the machine spin while the lid is open, use a stick to bypass the need for closing the lid. Insert the stick into the small hole which is meant to receive a lug on the lid when closed. Watch carefully as the tub begins to spin and the quilt moves out to the sides with centrifugal force. If at any time you need to adjust the distribution of the quilt, remove the stick to stop the spinning. Excessive spinning could cause creases in certain fabrics or battings.

If you have used detergent, rinse several times to remove all traces, refilling the tub without lifting the quilt.

After the final rinse and spin, remove the quilt from the machine, supporting it well underneath. Never put a quilt, old or new, in a clothes dryer. Do not hang a quilt to dry; the uneven strain will cause 'draping' (curving folds) between the clothespins, stretching the fabric irregularly. Instead, spread it flat with the top surface up. A floor with a clean sheet of plastic provides a suitably large surface. If a large floor area is not available, the quilt could also be spread on a bed covered with the sheet of plastic. Be sure the quilt, including the batt, is thoroughly dry before you put it away.

If you wish to do the washing in a bathtub, support the quilt on a large piece of plastic window screening. Do not remove the quilt from the water, but drain the tub with the quilt still in it. After washing and rinsing, leave the quilt to drain so it becomes less heavy. Then lift the screening to raise the quilt. Spread it flat and use clean towels to blot out excess water. Do not dry a quilt in the direct sun. Choose a day with lower humidity so the quilt will dry as quickly as possible. Drying can be accelerated with a hair dryer on low setting, or with a fan.

Storage

Once a quilt has been washed, most old fold lines should disappear. To avoid repetition of folds, rolling is the best storage method. See technical leaflets from the CCI for rolled storage and flat storage, which can work for smaller quilts.

Folds can be padded with acid-free tissue paper or well washed and rinsed old sheets. In some cases, sections of clean quilt batt material could be useful.

Display

If you want to display your quilt, other than on a bed, consider placing it over a padded bar, producing a soft roll with no folds. To present a quilt on a wall, Velcro works better than a cloth sleeve on a rod, because distortions and uneven hanging of quilts that are not square and straight can be corrected by realigning the Velcro. It is important not to tug at the quilt and cause damage when separating the two layers of Velcro to take down the quilt. A good method of attaching it is described in

CCI Note 13/4; be sure to use a strip of cotton fabric to mount the Velcro on the reverse of the quilt.

Too often, quilts displayed on walls are exposed to the deteriorating effects of handling, sunlight, heat from radiators, and smoke from cigarettes or fireplaces, and they will accumulate dust. Choose the display location to prevent these factors from affecting your treasured quilts. It is best to display a quilt for a short period only. Alternating quilts between display and storage allows the textiles to 'rest', thereby extending their life.

Labelling

For future generations, information about maker, date, pattern and origin should be attached to the reverse of a quilt, whether old or new. You can type information on a square of lightweight interfacing material and baste it to the backing fabric without having to turn the edges.

Photographing the Quilts

Photography was a major task in preparing the exhibition and book. Most of the quilts had been shot at one time or another, but there had never been a unified and consistent approach.

Quilts are challenging objects to photograph. Because of their size, they require a very large studio. They must be carefully spread with no draping or wrinkles, and, if possible, old fold lines should be eliminated (we used a professional steamer to relax the creases). To show the subtle quilting designs, sensitive and consistent lighting must be arranged.

Ron Merrick of Education Media Services, Department of Education, was the photographer for the project, assisted by Roger Lloyd. With many years of experience with museum artifacts, Ron approached the job with great enthusiasm. After studying the quality of quilt photography in many publications and determining the factors that were most important for us, we devised an approach we thought should work. Ron Merrick consulted several people on how they photographed quilts. Ken Burris of the Shelburne Museum, Vermont, had used a similar approach and was generous in providing several helpful tips.

We soon realized that our photography studio was too small for the quilt project. Fortunately, we were able to set up in a larger video studio. A support platform, about 3m x 3m (10′ x 10′), was constructed in the museum workshop using hollow-core doors. The platform was set up on a pulley system, so it could be raised and lowered. In the lowered position, we were able to spread the quilt out; the platform was then raised to an 80° angle. The camera (on a tripod) was set about 1 metre above the floor on a platform which could be moved backward and forward to accommodate various sizes of quilts. The camera was also set at an 80° angle, to eliminate distortion.

Black velvet (old studio curtains) was stretched to cover the quilt support platform and tacked down. There were two benefits in using this material. First, the black caused the space beyond the quilt to disappear in the photo. The results looked great in slide form, but produced difficulties in preparing for the book. Second, the velvet pile worked very well to prevent the quilts from slipping when nearly vertical. With the pile running

the 'wrong way', friction was increased. Only a few straight pins were needed to hold the edge of the quilt against the velvet-covered panel; silk backs posed the only difficulty, and required more pins.

Lighting required much experimentation. Careful consideration of the angle of light ensured that the quilting and subtle textures were evident. All of our quilts were photographed with the strongest illumination coming from the same relative position (with minor variation). The light fixtures were placed to the left because it is easier to interpret the relief of a quilted surface when shadow is cast from that side consistently. We placed the fixtures at a considerable distance from the quilts and lengthened the exposure time; this gave much more consistent results.

Even slightly unequal lighting over the whole surface of a large quilt can be distracting; we observed in published quilt photographs that our eyes more readily accepted light that dropped off from top to bottom rather than from side to side. Therefore, we placed the top of the quilt toward the left and lit from the left. In publication, the images are turned 90°, so that the light appears to come from the top.

Because of the time and space required for such work, it is worthwhile to consider taking a variety of images in several formats. We shot the whole collection in black-and-white as well as 35mm colour slides and larger colour transparencies, not knowing whether it would be possible to recreate the set-up in future.

Endnotes

Preface

[1] Marlene Davis, et al, *A Nova Scotia Work Basket*, 1976; Carter Houck, *Nova Scotia Patchwork Patterns*, 1981; Mern O'Brien, *Early Nova Scotia Quilts and Coverlets*, 1981; Roberta Horton, *Calico and Beyond*, 1986.

Introduction

[1] Ottawa: National Gallery of Canada, 1981, p. xii.

[2] With only one exception (Q 29), all of the quilts in the NSM collection are believed to have been made by women. In the documents examined, there is no reference to men quilting. However, boys are included in records of Junior Red Cross quilting in the 1940s and '50s.

[3] Jonathan Holstein, *American Pieced Quilts*, exhibition catalogue, 1972.

[4] Jonathan Holstein, *Quilts: An American Design Tradition*, 1973.

Chapter 1

[1] "Until the end of the eighteenth century English and American best quilts were very similar, fabrics for tops being exported from England, and even after the War of Independence, England was the source of taste and design for well-to-do Americans." Shiela Betterton, *The American Quilt Tradition*, 1976, p. 5

[2] To some extent, American block patterns also crossed to Britain in the late 1800s. As well, decorative crazy quilts and log cabin quilts were popular on both sides of the Atlantic. In Britain, log cabin constuction was sometimes identified as 'American' or 'Canadian quilting'. S. Caulfeild & B. Saward, *The Dictionary of Needlework*, London, 1882.

Chapter 2

[1] A distinction must be made between the Acadian farmers and the French who were stationed at Fortress Louisbourg, as representatives of the French government. The Acadians had developed their own independent culture based on living in North America. Nevertheless, an important area for further research will be the Louisbourg estate records. Approximately 130 out of 155 inventories have been transcribed from microfilm records in France. In a small sampling, three out of five list quilts. In a paper prepared by Blaine Adams, *The Construction and Occupation of the Barracks of the King's Bastion* (Fortress of Louisbourg National Historic Site, 1974), there are seven references to quilts in a sampling of inventories dated from 1732 to 1753, representative of different social classes at the fortress. Undoubtedly the most impressive quilt would have been one in the household of Jean-Baptiste-Louis le Prévost Duquesnel. He was Governor of the French colony of Isle Royale (Cape Breton) and commandant of the fortress of Louisbourg between 1740 and 1744. On his bed was "une courtepointe piqué[e] de taffetas blanc". The bed canopy was also trimmed with white quilted taffeta. Several other inventories list "courtepointes d'indienne piquées", suggesting that quilted palampores were in relatively common use in France in the mid-1700s.

[2] Several currencies were in use in Nova Scotia at the time: English pounds sterling, 'New York' dollars, and 'Montreal' dollars, among others.

[3] For background history, see *No Place Like Home: Diaries and Letters of Nova Scotia Women, 1771-1938*, by Margaret Conrad, Toni Laidlaw, and Donna Smyth, p. 6.

[4] The Black Historical and Educational Research Organization (HERO) project (unpublished material) was carried out in Black communities through-out the province in the early 1970s.

[5] M. Conrad, T. Laidlaw, and D. Smyth, *No Place Like Home*, p. 29.

[6] In the late 1960s, shipping costs began to escalate and it was no longer practical to send quilts abroad; the Red Cross redirected its efforts towards producing quilts to be sold or raffled, thereby raising money for overseas relief. Nevertheless, women still make Red Cross 'disaster' quilts for victims of local fires or floods.

[7] *Canadian Mosaic: Nova Scotia Volume*, complied by Mrs W.A. Turner, Women's Institutes of Nova Scotia, 1957.

Chapter 3

[1] An exception was the Victoria and Albert Museum which published a small booklet in 1938, *Notes on Applied Work and Patchwork*. While interested in early examples, this booklet did not encourage anyone to study later work: "Patchwork of the late 19th century deserves no more than a passing mention; it was made from scraps purchased at the dressmaker's and generally speaking is deplorable both in colour and design", p. 10. The Victoria and Albert Museum had previously published *Notes on Quilting*, in 1932.

[2] Elizabeth Hake, *English Quilting: Old and New*, 1937; Agnes M. Miall, *Patchwork Old and New*, 1937.

[3] Mavis FitzRandolph, *Traditional Quilting: Its Story and Its Practice*, 1954; Averil Colby, *Patchwork Quilts*, 1965.

[4] Marion Robertson wrote of this in *The Chestnut Pipe: Folklore of Shelburne County*. A follow-up phone call to the woman who knew of the newspaper-filled quilt confirmed the story.

[5] See Pat L. Nickol's article "The Use of Cotton Sacks in Quiltmaking", in *Uncoverings, 1988*, as well as Merikay Waldvogel's *Soft Covers for Hard Times: Quiltmaking & the Great Depression*.

[6] Neither would conservators recommend the method used at Mount Uniacke in the 1930s. According to a maid who worked at the house, quilts were washed in Lake Martha, adjacent to the house. They were then towed behind a canoe to rinse. Interview, 1990, with Dorothy (Shunamon) O'Leary who worked as a maid for Mrs Cobbett (Helena Victoria Uniacke), who supervised the opening of the house each summer.

Chapter 4

[1] Agnes Miall advised using this method, in *Patchwork Old and New*, 1937. Making a windmill block, she says "Having obtained your pattern, you must decide whether you will piece with or without backing papers", but recommends it "except for the simplest designs"; p. 69-70.

[2] A man from Newfoundland offered an explanation of this term, noting the similarity with the diamond shapes produced when a fishing net is hung from the edge of the mesh, suspended on a line running parallel to the surface of the water.

[3] Valerie Wilson, "Quiltmaking in Counties Antrim and Down: Some Preliminary Findings from the Ulster Quilt Survey", in *Uncoverings, 1991*, vol. 12, p. 150.

Appendix 1

[1] c/o Canadian Museums Association, Suite 400, 280 Metcalfe Street, Ottawa, Ontario, K2P 1R7

[2] 1030 Innes Road, Ottawa, Ontario, K1A 0M5

Comments from textile specialists at the CCI, especially Ela Keyserlingk and Joan Marshall, were helpful in preparing this section.

Primary Sources

abbreviations

BA - Baptist Archives, Acadia University, Wolfville
DA - Diocesan Archives (Anglican Church), Halifax
MCA - Maritime Conference Archives (United Church), Halifax
NSM - Nova Scotia Museum, Halifax
PANS - Public Archives of Nova Scotia, Halifax
UCCB - University College of Cape Breton, Sydney

Church Group Records

Aylesford; Methodist Church Ladies Aid, 1917 to 1934; MCA
Barrington Passage; St. James United Church, Ladies Aid Society, minute books, 1923 to 1939; MCA
Barss Corner; Methodist Church, Ladies Aid Society, minutes, 1913 to 1930; MCA
Halfway Brook; Ladies Aid, minute book 1926 to 1930; PANS Micro
Halfway Brook; Ladies Aid, record books, 1937 to 1950; PANS Micro
Halifax; Brunswick Street United Church, scrapbook, c. 1923 to 1947; MCA
Halifax; Jost Mission Committee, annual reports, 1921 to 1948; PANS
Halifax (Fairview); Friendly Circle of Community Sunday School; MCA
Lower Horton; Auxiliary of the Nova Scotia Branch of the Woman's Missionary Society of the Methodist Church, 1911; MCA
Marion Bridge; United Church Ladies Aid, minutes, 1939 to 1951; MCA
Middle Musquodoboit, Middleton United Church, minute book, July 1944 to January 1947; MCA
Middle Musquodoboit; Middleton Church Sewing Circle, 12 May 1897 to 30 December 1920; MCA
Middle Musquodoboit; Middleton Church Sewing Circle, minute book 2, 1921 to 1929; MCA
Middle Musquodoboit; Middleton Church Sewing Circle, minute book, 30 January 1930 to 29 August 1940; MCA
Middle Musquodoboit; Middleton Ladies Aid/Woman's Association, treasurer's records, January 1944 to December 1954; MCA
Milton; Christian Church, Loyal Women's Council, Church of Christ's Disciples, minute book; BA
Mulgrave; Women's Auxiliary of the Parish of St. Andrew's Anglican Church, minute book, 1913 to 1925; DA
Nova Scotia Branch of the Women's Auxiliary to the Missionary Society of the Church of England in Canada, Diocesan Mission Board, minute book, December 1921 to April 1926; DA
Port Williams; Baptist Church, "Loyal Workers" Sunday School Class; BA
Sambro; Sewing Circle, minutes, 1921 to 1924 ; MCA
Upper Granville; Woman's Auxiliary of the Parish of St. James Anglican Church, minute book, 1914 to 1920, and Red Cross minutes, 1944; DA
Wolfville; United Baptist Church, Social & Benevolent Society, 1940 to 1943; BA

The Missionary Register, vol. 10, no. 10, October 1859; PANS
The Presbyterian Witness (1848 to 1925), 1879, 1899-1890, 1900, 1911, 1925; MCA
The United Churchman, 1931; MCA

Diaries

Bell, Almira; 1833 to 1836, Barrington; PANS
Campbell, Susan Dunlop; 1879 to 1925; private collection see article by George Campbell, "Susan Dunlop: Her Diary" in *Dalhousie Review*, summer 1966, vol. 46 no. 2, p. 215-222
Ells, Rebecca; 1896 to 1904; BA
Gill, Sara (Gammon); 1888; PANS
Michener, Margaret (Dickie); 1840s to 1869; PANS (in *The Acadian*, mid-1920s to 24 May 1928)

Norris, Mary Ann; 1818 to 1839; PANS
Seaman, Amos 'King'; 1840 to 1864; Charles Bruce Fergusson, "The Old King is Back: Amos 'King' Seaman and his Diary", The Public Archives of Nova Scotia, *Bulletin* no. 23, Halifax, 1972
Smith, Mary Elizabeth (Wood); March 1891 to May 1892; UCCB
Wetmore, Alice; 1902 to 1903; Yarmouth County Museum Archives
Winslow, Anna Green; 1771 to 1772; in *Diary of Anna Green Winslow, A Boston School Girl of 1771*, edited by Alice Morse Earle; Williamstown, Massachusetts: Corner House Publishers, 1894; reprinted 1974
Winton, Mary; April 1892 to June 1893; UCCB

Exhibition Records

1851; Exhibition of the Works of Industry of All Nations, London, reports by the juries; NSM library
1854; Nova Scotia Industrial Exhibition, MS list; PANS
1862; International Exhibition, London, Report of the Nova Scotia Commissioners; PANS
1867; Paris Exhibition, Catalogue of the Nova Scotia Department; PANS
1876; International Exhibition, Philadelphia, Catalogue of the British Section; PANS
1878; Agricultural and Industrial Exhibition, Truro, prize list; PANS
1882; Annual District Exhibition for the Counties of Digby, Yarmouth and Shelburne, Yarmouth, prize list; PANS
1886; Colonial and Indian Exhibition, London, catalogue; PANS
1907; Hants, Kings and Annapolis Counties' Fruit and Poultry Exhibition, Windsor, prize list; PANS
1935; Windsor Exhibition, prize list; PANS
1939; Nova Scotia Provincial Exhibition, files; PANS MG 20 vol. 739, MG 20, vol. 740, #72
1939; Nova Scotia Provincial Exhibition, files; PANS MG 20, vol. 737, #9
1945, 1946, 1949, 1951; Craftsmen-at-Work Exhibition, catalogues; PANS
1960; Nova Scotia Provincial Exhibition, prize list; PANS
1963; Nova Scotia Provincial Exhibition, Handcraft Division, Truro, report; PANS
1964, 1967, 1969, 1978, 1980, 1982, 1985; Hants County Exhibition, prize lists; PANS
1967; Atlantic Pavilion for Expo '67, records; PANS RG 43, #1

N.S. Provincial Exhibition, files; PANS MG 20 vol. 1311, #22

Bridgewater Bulletin, 14 October 1902; PANS
The Enterprise, New Glasgow, 11 October 1890; PANS
Liverpool Advance, 6 October 1880; PANS
Yarmouth Light, 1 & 7 October 1896; PANS

Inventories

c1720 to c1760; French, various; Fortress Louisbourg, Cape Breton; Parks Canada Library
1772; Mrs Martha Harrington, Newport, 24 November 1772; PANS micro reel #19561, Hants County
1777; Mrs Catherine Brennock, Halifax, 30 September and October 1777; PANS micro #19398
1782; Philip Knaut, Lunenburg, 4 June 1782; PANS micro #19411
1785; Robert Harding, 3 May 1785; PANS micro #20166, Shelburne County
1786; Capt. Abraham Knowlton, Cornwallis, 12 August 1786; PANS micro #19411
1789; John Wardell, Shelburne, 14 February 1789; PANS micro #20166, Shelburne County
1797; Joshua Ells, Cornwallis, 26 January 1797; PANS micro #19738, Kings County
1800; Capt. Robert Wirling, Shelburne, 28 October and 4 December 1800; NSM
1803; David Eaton, Cornwallis, 21 July 1803; PANS micro #19738, Kings County

1803; W. Shineff Handfield, Halifax, 12 September 1803; PANS micro #19407, Halifax County

1804; Henry Aiken, Halifax, 31 May 1804; PANS micro #19396, Halifax County

1809; Jonathan Anderson, 13 October 1809, PANS micro #19004, Annapolis County

1810; Casper Wollenhaupt, 12 January 1810; PANS micro #19842, Lunenburg County

1812; James Eaton, 30 May 1812; PANS micro #19738, Kings County

1812; William Birch Brinley, Halifax, 1812; PANS micro #19398

1817; George Dewolf, Windsor, 2 June 1817; NSM

1819; William Lee, Halifax, 31 August 1819; PANS micro #19411, Halifax County

1827; Mary Anderson, 8 September 1827; PANS micro #19004, Annapolis County

1829; William Annand, 7 July 1829; PANS micro #19396, Halifax County

1830; Richard John Uniacke, Mount Uniacke, 17-18 November 1830; NSM

1837; Isaac Anderson, 4 September 1837; PANS micro #19004, Annapolis County

1846; Samuel Lawrence, Halifax, June 1846; PANS micro #19411, Halifax County

1870; Ward Eaton, Cornwallis, 24 February 1870; PANS micro #19738, Kings County

1871; James Alexander, July 1871; PANS micro #19004, Annapolis County

1882; Whitman Armstrong, 21 December 1882; PANS micro #19004, Annapolis County

Magazines and Catalogues

Atlantic Weekly, 5 September 1896

Chatelaine, 1920s and 1930s

T. Eaton Co., *Catalogue*, 1900, 1902, 1905-6, 1911-12, 1912-13, 1920-21, 1921-22, and assorted to 1976

The Family Herald and Weekly Star, 1920s to 1940s; Nova Scotia Agricultural College archives

The Farmer Magazine, May 1937; PANS

The Maritime Farmer, 1920s and 1930s; Nova Scotia Agricultural College archives

Montgomery Ward & Co., *Catalogue #57*, 1895

Needlecraft, 1920s and 1930s; NSM

Robert Simpson Co. Ltd., *Catalogue*, 1905 to 1970s

Sears, Roebuck and Co., *Catalogue #104*, 1897

Weekend Magazine, Harry Bruce, "The Women of Nova Scotia Know Something Their Mothers Didn't...", 16 February 1974

Miscellaneous Historical Material

Alexander Graham Bell Club, Baddeck, Minute Book, 1926; AGB Club records

Armstrong, Mary (1867-1949), family memoir; private collection

Cosy Hour Club, Oakland, Lunenburg County, minute books, June 1955 to June 1956, and May 1957 to May 1963; private collection

Female academies, circular (n.d.) and advertisement (1856); PANS RG 14 vol. 45F, #4 and #9 (Berringer collection)

Provincial Hospital for the Insane, Halifax, Report of the Medical Superintendent, 1865, publ. 1866; PANS

Quilt patterns from newspapers and magazines, undated scrapbook; private collection

Robinson, John, and Thomas Rispin, *Journey Through Nova Scotia*, 1774; PANS, reprinted in *N.S. Archives Reports*, 1944

Seaman family correspondence; private collection

Newsletters and Newspapers

Atlantic Canada Newspaper Survey, for period prior to 1800; Canadian Heritage Information Network (CHIN) database

Dartmouth Patriot, 1916; Dartmouth Public Library micro

The Halifax Daily Report and Times, 2 January 1878

Handcraft Centre Bulletin, March 1975 to June/July 1977; Halifax City Regional Library

Handcrafts, January 1944 to January 1973; PANS TT1 H236

N.S. Designer Craftsmen, newsletter, May 1973 to December 1975; PANS

The Presbyterian Witness, 27 April 1867

Oral Histories

Black Historical and Educational Research Organization (HERO) Oral History Project, 1970s; private collection

Nova Scotia Museum Oral History Project, Jeddore Oyster Ponds, 1981; NSM Library

Ross Farm Oral History Project, 1982; NSM Library

Red Cross Records

Canadian Red Cross Society, Nova Scotia Division, Annual Reports, 1915 to 1990

Canadian Red Cross Society, Musquodoboit Valley Branch, executive minutes; PANS MG 20 1367 #16

Junior Red Cross Newsletter, Nova Scotia, 1938 to 1953; PANS HV 583 C212 N935

Women's Institutes of N.S. and 4-H Records

The Acadian, 'For Home and Country' page, 15 November 1928; PANS

Cape Breton County Farmers Association, exhibition committee minutes; UCCB

4-H Club News, assorted issues from 1966 through 1970s and 1980s

Habitant; Women's Institute, minutes, random selections 1935 and 1938; PANS MG 20 vol. 950

Halfway Brook; Women's Institute, minute book, 1922 to 1924; PANS MG 20 vol. 953

Hantsport; Women's Institute, minutes; PANS MG 20 vol. 1134

Home and Country newsletter, Women's Institutes of Nova Scotia, Truro, July 1923 to March-April 1952

Otter Brook; Women's Institute, minutes, 1953; PANS MG 20 vol. 953

Shepard, Mary, et al., "Reflections: A History of the Homeville Branch of the Women's Institutes of Nova Scotia", Homeville, Cape Breton Co., 1983; UCCB

West Brook and Halfway River; Women's Institutes of Nova Scotia; PANS MG 4 #181

Women's Institutes of Nova Scotia, records; WINS office, Truro

Secondary Sources

Adams, Blaine. *The Construction and Occupation of the Barracks of the King's Bastion.* Fortress Louisbourg, N.S.: unpubl. paper, 1974

Baron De Hirsch Congregation, 1890 to 1990. Halifax: Beth Israel Synagogue, 1990

Bass River Village History, 1765-1955. Bass River, N.S.: Women's Institutes of Nova Scotia, 1955

Brown, Harry, and others. *Lore of North Cumberland.* Hantsport, N.S.: Lancelot Press, North Cumberland Historical Society, 1982

Bull, Mary Kate. *Sandy Cove: The History of a Nova Scotia Village.* Hantsport, N.S.: Lancelot Press, 1978

Burnett, Augusta Benvie. *Newton Mills and Other Stories.* Upper Stewiacke, N.S.: 1973

Burrows, Mildred Pulsifer. *A History of Wittenburg (St. Andrews).* 1962

Canadian Mosaic: Nova Scotia Volume, compiled by Mrs W.A. Turner. Women's Institutes of Nova Scotia, 1957

Cobequid Chronicles: A Brief History of Truro and Vicinity. Truro, N.S.: University Women's Club of Truro, 1975

Conrad, Margaret, Toni Laidlaw, and Donna Smyth. *No Place Like Home: Diaries and Letters of Nova Scotia Women 1771-1938.* Halifax: Formac Publ. Co. Ltd, 1988

Davison, James Doyle, ed. *Mud Creek: The Story of the Town of Wolfville, Nova Scotia.* Wolfville, N.S.: Wolfville Historical Society, 1985

DesBrisay, M.B. *History of the County of Lunenburg.* Bridgewater, N.S.: Bridgewater Bulletin, 1967, 3rd ed. (first pub. 1870)

Deveau, J. Alphonse. *Along the Shores of Saint Mary's Bay: the Story of a Unique Community.* Church Point, N.S.: Imprimerie de l'Université, 1977

Deyarmond, E.M. *The Whip-Handle Tree.* Kentville, N.S.: Kentville Publishing Co., n.d.

Duncanson, John Victor. *Newport, Nova Scotia: A Rhode Island Township.* Belleville, Ontario: Mika Publishing Co., 1985

Forsythe, G.E. *More Tales of the Yesteryears, Book Two: the Writings of Mrs E.S. Williams, East Jeddore, 1888-1979.* 1980

Gillis, Yvonne. "The Art of Quilting", unpub. paper, n.d.; UCCB

Glabay, Margaret. "Crafts in Cape Breton 1900-1989", unpub. paper, n.d.; UCCB

Goddard, Hazel Firth. *Retracing Steps in Shelburne County.* Dartmouth, N.S.: Seashell, 1990

Green, H. Gordon, ed., and Federated Women's Institutes of Canada. *A Heritage of Canadian Handcrafts.* Toronto: McClelland & Stewart Ltd., 1967

Hartling, Philip L. *Where Broad Atlantic Surges Roll.* Antigonish, N.S.: Formac Publishing Co., 1979

An Historical Sketch of the Provincial Chapter of Nova Scotia IODE, 1920-1980. PANS HQ1909 N935 I34

A History of Noel Shore. Women's Institute, Noel Shore Branch, c1981

History of Port Clyde. Port Clyde Women's Institute. Shelburne, N.S.: South Shore Gazette Ltd., 1954

A History of the Village of Sherbrooke and Vicinity, compiled and written by Women's Institute, 1947

The Islands Look Back. Cape Sable Island, N.S.: Archelaus Smith Historical Society, 1981

Jennex, Helen M. *Rambling Memories.* 1977

Jennex, Helen M. *Reminiscence.* 1976

Kendrick, Mary F. *Down the Road to Yesterday: A History of Springfield, Annapolis County, N.S.* Bridgewater, N.S.: 1941

Langille, Birdie Kaulbach. *And Now We Remember, History of Barss Corner, Lunenburg County, N.S.* [1971?]

Mackley, M. Florence. *Handweaving in Cape Breton.* Sydney, N.S.: privately printed, 1967

Messenger, Margaret E. *Our Island's Bygone Days.* Cape Sable Island, N.S.: Archelaus Smith Historical Society, 1988

Morris, W.S.H. "The Nova Scotia Country-Side One Hundred Years Ago or Scraps from Memory's Rag-Bag", in *Collections of the Nova Scotia Historical Society,* vol. 25, 1942

Over the Mountain and Down to the Bay. Margaretsville Women's Institute, 1992

Phillips, Adora. *A History of Bishopville, Kings County, Nova Scotia, 1710-1974.* [1975?]

Richardson, Evelyn. *We Keep a Light.* Toronto: Ryerson Press, 1945

Robertson, Marion. *The Chestnut Pipe: Folklore of Shelburne County.* Halifax: Nimbus Publishing, 1991

60 Years of Learning by Doing, 1922-1982. Nova Scotia 4-H Council, 1982

Through the Years: The Women's Institute Story, A History of W.I.N.S., 1913-1979. Women's Institutes of Nova Scotia, 1980

Veinotte, Pauline M. *Newburne—Then and Now.* Bridgewater, N.S.: Langille's Print, 1989

Wilson, Helen Dacey. *More Tales from Barrett's Landing.* Toronto: McClelland & Stewart Ltd., 1967

Selected Books and Articles on Quilts

Oshins, Lisa Turner, compiler. *Quilt Collections: A Directory for the United States and Canada.* Washington, D.C.: Acropolis Books Ltd., 1987

Makowski, Colleen Lahan. *Quilting, 1915-1983: An Annotated Bibliography.* Metuchen, New Jersey: Scarecrow Press Inc., 1985

Nova Scotia

Davis, Marlene, Joanne Creelman, Joleen Gordon, Mary Roddis, Mary Saunders, & Doris Wentzell. *A Nova Scotia Work Basket: Some Needlework Patterns Traditionally Used in the Province.* Halifax, N.S.: Nova Scotia Museum, 1976

Houck, Carter. *Nova Scotia Patchwork Patterns,* with instructions and full-size templates for 12 quilts. New York: Dover Publications Inc., 1981

O'Brien, Mern. *Early Nova Scotia Quilts and Coverlets.* Exhib. catalogue. Halifax, N.S.: Dalhousie University Art Gallery, 1981

Robson, Scott. "Learning More about Quilts", 5 articles, in *The Occasional,* Halifax, N.S.: Nova Scotia Museum, 1979-1982
  Part I: "Useful Reference Books", vol. 5, no. 3, spring 1979
  Part II a: "What Is a Quilt?", vol. 6, no. 1, fall 1979
  Part II b: "Types of Quilts and Quilting Terms", vol. 6, no. 2, fall 1980
  Part III a: "Pieced Quilts", vol. 6, no. 3, spring 1981
  Part III b: "Pieced Quilts", vol. 7, no. 2, spring 1982

Robson, Scott. "Textiles in Nova Scotia" in *Spirit of Nova Scotia: Traditional Decorative Folk Art, 1780-1930.* Halifax, N.S.: Art Gallery of Nova Scotia, 1985; with Dundurn Press, Toronto & London

Canada

Burnham, Dorothy K. *Pieced Quilts of Ontario.* Toronto: Royal Ontario Museum, 1975

Conroy, Mary. *300 Years of Canada's Quilts.* Toronto: Griffin House, 1976

McKendry, Ruth. *Quilts and Other Bed Coverings in the Canadian Tradition.* Toronto: Van Nostrand Reinhold, 1979. (Published in New York as *Traditional Quilts and Bedcoverings.*)

Patterson, Nancy-Lou. "Log Cabin Quilts", in *Canadian Collector,* Nov./Dec., 1977, p. 40-44

Great Britain

Allan, Rosemary E. *North Country Quilts and Coverlets from Beamish Museum, County Durham.* Beamish, England: The North of England Open Air Museum, 1987

Anthony, Ilid E. "Quilting and Patchwork in Wales" in *Amgueddfa* (Bulletin of The National Museum of Wales), no. 12, winter 1972, p. 2-15

Caulfeild, Sophia Frances Anne, & Blanche C. Saward. *The Dictionary of Needlework.* London: 1882; reprint of 1887 edition by Dover Publication Inc., New York, 1972, as *Encyclopedia of Victorian Needlework*

Clabburn, Pamela. *The Needleworker's Dictionary.* New York: W. Morrow & Co. Inc., 1976

Clabburn, Pamela. *Patchwork.* (Shire album 101). Aylesbury, Bucks, U.K.: Shire Publications Ltd., 1983

Colby, Averil. *Patchwork.* London: B.T. Batsford Ltd., 1958

Colby, Averil. *Patchwork Quilts.* London: B.T. Batsford Ltd., 1965; reprinted 1988

Colby, Averil. *Quilting.* London: B.T. Batsford Ltd., 1972; reprinted 1987

FitzRandolph, Mavis, & Florence M. Fletcher. *Quilting: Traditional Methods and Design.* Leicester, England: Dryad Press, second edition 1960 (copyright 1955)

FitzRandolph, Mavis. *Traditional Quilting: Its Story and Its Practice.* London: B.T. Batsford, 1954

Freeman, June. *Quilting, Patchwork and Appliqué, 1700-1982: Sewing as a Woman's Art.* Exhib. catalogue. Colchester, England: Art at The Minories, 1982; also London: Crafts Council Gallery, 1983

Hake, Elizabeth. *English Quilting: Old and New, with Notes on Its West Country Tradition.* New York: Charles Scribner's Sons, & London: B.T. Batsford, 1937; reprinted 1988

Meldrum, Alex. *Irish Patchwork.* Dublin, Ireland: Kilkenny Design Workshops, 1979. Ex. cat., with an introduction by Laura Jones

Miall, Agnes M. *Patchwork Old and New.* London: The Woman's Magazine Office, 1937

Osler, Dorothy. *Traditional British Quilts.* London: B.T. Batsford, 1987

Parker, Freda. *Victorian Patchwork.* London: Anaya Publishers Ltd., 1991

Parry, Linda. *The Practical Guide to Patchwork from The Victoria & Albert Collection.* London: Unwin Hyman, 1987

Rae, Janet. *The Quilts of the British Isles.* New York: E.P. Dutton, 1987; also London: Constable, 1987

Victoria & Albert Museum. *Notes on Applied Work and Patchwork.* London: Victoria and Albert Museum, 1938 and 1949

Victoria & Albert Museum. *Notes on Quilting.* London: Victoria and Albert Museum, 1960 (first publ. 1932)

United States

Atkins, Jacqueline M., & Phyllis Tepper. *New York Beauties: Quilts from the Empire State.* New York: Dutton Studio Books, in association with The Museum of American Folk Art, 1992

Benberry, Cuesta. "Afro-American Women and Quilts: An Introductory Essay", in *Uncoverings*, vol. 1, 1980

Benberry, Cuesta; forewords by Jonathan Holstein & Shelly Zegart. *Always There: The African-American Presence in American Quilts.* Louisville, Kentucky: The Kentucky Quilt Project Inc., 1992

Betterton, Shiela. *More Quilts and Coverlets from The American Museum in Britain.* Bath, U.K.: The American Museum in Britain, 1989

Betterton, Shiela. *Quilts and Coverlets from The American Museum in Britain.* Bath, U.K.: The American Museum in Britain, 1978; reprinted 1982

Betterton, Shiela. *The American Quilt Tradition.* Exhib. catalogue. Bath, U.K.: The American Museum in Britain, 1976

Binney, Edwin III, & Gail Winslow-Binney. *Homage to Amanda: Two Hundred Years of American Quilts from the Collection of Edwin Binney, 3rd, and Gail Binney Winslow.* San Francisco, California: R.K. Press, with the Smithsonian Institution Traveling Exhibition Service (SITES) & the San Diego Museum of Art

Bishop, Robert, & Patricia Coblentz. *New Discoveries in American Quilts.* New York: E.P. Dutton & Co. Inc., 1975

Bonfield, Lynn A. "Diaries of New England Quilters before 1860", in *Uncoverings*, vol. 9, 1988

Brackman, Barbara. "A Chronological Index to Pieced Quilt Patterns, 1775-1825", in *Uncoverings*, vol. 4, 1983

Brackman, Barbara. "Dating Antique Quilts: 200 Years of Style, Pattern and Technique", Technical Guide #4. San Francisco: American Quilt Study Group, 1990

Brackman, Barbara. "Signature Quilts: Nineteenth-Century Trends", in *Uncoverings*, vol. 10, 1989

Brackman, Barbara. "The Strip Tradition in European-American Quilts", in *The Clarion*, New York: Museum of American Folk Art, fall 1989, p. 45

Brackman, Barbara. *An Encyclopedia of Pieced Quilt Patterns.* vol. 1-8. Lawrence, Kansas: Prairie Flower Publications, 1979-1984 (reprinted in one vol. by the American Quilter's Society, Paducah, Kentucky, 1993)

Brackman, Barbara. *Clues in the Calico: A Guide to Identifying and Dating Antique Quilts.* McLean, Virginia: EPM Publications Inc., 1989

Bullard, Lacy Folmar, & Betty Jo Shiell. *Chintz Quilts: Unfading Glory.* Tallahassee, Florida: Serendipity Publishers, 1983

Carlisle, Lilian Baker. *Pieced Work and Appliqué Quilts at Shelburne Museum.* Shelburne, Vermont: Shelburne Museum Publications, 1957

Cleveland, Richard L., & Donna Bister. *Plain and Fancy: Vermont's People and Their Quilts as a Reflection of America.* Gualala, California: The Quilt Digest Press, 1991

Cooper, Patricia, & Norma Bradley Buferd. *The Quilters: Women and Domestic Art.* Garden City, N.Y.: Anchor Press/ Doubleday, 1978

Cozart, Dorothy. "A Century of Fundraising Quilts: 1860-1960", in *Uncoverings*, vol. 5, 1984

Cozart, Dorothy. "When the Smoke Cleared", in *The Quilt Digest*, no. 5. San Francisco, California: The Quilt Digest Press, 1987, p. 50-57

Dunton, William, Jr., M.D. *Old Quilts.* Catonsville, Maryland: the author, 1946

Ferrero, Pat, Elaine Hedges, & Julia Silber. *Hearts and Hands: The Influence of Women & Quilts on American Society.* San Francisco, California: Quilt Digest Press, 1987

Finley, Ruth E. *Old Patchwork Quilts, and the Women Who Made Them.* Philadelphia & London: J.B. Lippincott, 1929; reprinted by Charles T. Brandford Co., Newton Center, Mass., 1970

Fox, Sandi. *Small Endearments: 19th-Century Quilts for Children.* New York: Charles Scribner's Sons, 1985

Fox, Sandi. *Wrapped in Glory: Figurative Quilts & Bedcovers, 1700-1900.* New York: Thames & Hudson Inc., with the Los Angeles County Museum of Art, 1990

Garoutte, Sally. "Early Colonial Quilts in a Bedding Context", in *Uncoverings*, vol. 1, 1980

Gunn, Virginia. "Crazy Quilts and Outline Quilts: Popular Responses to the Decorative Art/Art Needlework Movement, 1876-1893", in *Uncoverings*, vol. 5, 1984

Gunn, Virginia. "Victorian Silk Template Patchwork in American Periodicals, 1850-1875", in *Uncoverings*, vol. 4, 1983

Hall, Carrie A., & Rose G. Kretsinger. *The Romance of the Patchwork Quilt in America.* Caldwell, Idaho: Caxton Printers Ltd., 1935, reprinted by Bonanza Books, New York, n.d.

Hersh, Tandy. "18th-Century Quilted Silk Petticoats Worn in America", in *Uncoverings*, vol. 5, 1984

Holstein, Jonathan. "Collecting Quilt Data: History from Statistics", in *The Quilt Digest*, no. 1. San Francisco, California: Kirakofe & Kile, 1983, p. 62-69

Holstein, Jonathan. *Abstract Design in American Quilts.* Exhib. catalogue. New York: Whitney Museum of American Art, 1971

Holstein, Jonathan. *American Pieced Quilts.* Exhib. catalogue. Washington, D.C.: Renwick Gallery of The National Collection of Fine Arts, Smithsonian Institution, 1972

Holstein, Jonathan. *The Pieced Quilt: An American Design Tradition.* Greenwich, Connecticut: New York Graphic Society Ltd., 1973

Houck, Carter. *The Quilt Encyclopedia Illustrated.* New York: Harry N. Abrams Inc., with The Museum of American Folk Art, 1991

Ickis, Marguerite. *The Standard Book of Quilt Making and Collecting.* New York: Dover Publications Inc., 1959; previously published by Greystone Press, New York, 1949

Johnson, Bruce. *A Child's Comfort: Baby and Doll Quilts in American Folk Art.* New York & London: Harcourt Brace Jovanovich, 1977

Khin, Yvonne M. *The Collector's Dictionary of Quilt Names and Patterns.* New York: Portland House, 1988 (published in 1980 by Acropolis Books, Washington, D.C.)

Kile, Michael M., & Roderick Kiracofe, editors. *The Quilt Digest.* San Francisco, California: Kiracofe & Kile, 1983-84, and The Quilt Digest Press, 1985-87

Kimball, Jeana. *Red and Green: An Appliqué Tradition.* Bothell, Washington: That Patchwork Place Inc., 1990

Kiracofe, Roderick, with Mary Elizabeth Johnson. *The American Quilt: A History of Cloth and Comfort, 1750-1950.* New York: Clarkson Potter, 1993

Kirkpatrick, Emma. "Quilts, Quiltmaking and the *Progressive Farmer*, 1886-1935", in *Uncoverings*, vol. 6, 1985

Kolter, Jane Bentley. *Forget Me Not: A Gallery of Friendship and Album Quilts.* Pittstown, New Jersey: The Main Street Press, 1985

Koob, Katherine R. "Documenting Quilts by Their Fabrics", in *Uncoverings*, vol. 2, 1981

Lane, Rose Wilder. *Woman's Day Book of American Needlework.* New York: Simon & Schuster, 1963 [columns from *Woman's Day* magazine 1961-1963]

Lasansky, Jeannette. *Bits and Pieces: Textile Traditions.* Lewisburg, Pennsylvania: Oral Traditions Project of the Union County Historical Society, 1991

Lasansky, Jeannette. *In the Heart of Pennsylvania: 19th & 20th Century Quiltmaking Traditions.* Lewisburg, Pennsylvania: Oral Traditions Project of the Union County Historical Society, 1985

Lasansky, Jeannette. *Pieced by Mother: Over 100 Years of Quiltmaking Traditions.* Lewisburg, Pennsylvania: Oral Traditions Project of the Union County Historical Society, 1987

Lasansky, Jeannette. *Pieced by Mother: Symposium Papers.* Lewisburg, Pennsylvania: Oral Traditions Project of the Union County Historical Society, 1988

Laury, Jean Ray, & the California Heritage Quilt Project. *Ho for California!: Pioneer Women and Their Quilts.* New York: E.P. Dutton, 1990.

Lipsett, Linda O. *Remember Me: Women and Their Friendship Quilts.* Quilt Digest Press: 1985, revised edition 1989.

McKim, Ruby Short. *One Hundred and One Patchwork Patterns.* New York: Dover Publications Inc., 1962; originally published by McKim Studios, Independence, Missouri, 1931

McMorris, Penny. *Crazy Quilts.* New York: E.P. Dutton Inc., 1984

Meyer, Suellen. "Early Influences of the Sewing Machine and Visible Machine Stitching on Nineteenth-Century Quilts", in *Uncoverings*, vol. 10, 1989

Nickols, Pat L. "The Use of Cotton Sacks in Quiltmaking", in *Uncoverings*, vol. 9, 1988

Nylander, Jane C. "Flowers from the needle", in *An American Sampler: Folk Art from the Shelburne Museum.* Exhib. catalogue. Washington, D.C.: National Gallery of Art, 1987

Oliver, Celia Y. *Fifty-Five Famous Quilts from the Shelburne Museum in Full Color.* New York: Dover Publications Inc., & Shelburne Museum, 1990

Orlofsky, Patsy, & Myron Orlofsky. *Quilts in America.* New York & Toronto, etc.: McGraw-Hill Book Company, 1974 (reprinted 1992 by Abbeville Press)

Peaden, Joyce B. "Donated Quilts Warmed Wartorn Europe", in *Uncoverings*, vol. 9, 1988

Peck, Amelia. *American Quilts & Coverlets in The Metropolitan Museum of Art.* New York: The Metropolitan Museum of Art, & Dutton Studio Books, 1990

Peto, Florence. *American Quilts and Coverlets: A History of a Charming Native Art Together with a Manual of Instruction for Beginners.* New York: Chanticleer Press, 1949

Peto, Florence. *Historic Quilts.* New York: American Historical Co. Inc., 1939

Ramsey, Bets, & Merikay Waldvogel. *The Quilts of Tennessee: Images of Domestic Life Prior to 1930.* Nashville, Tennessee: Rutledge Hill Press, 1986

Rehmel, Judy. *The Quilt ID Book: 4,000 Illustrated and Indexed patterns.* New York: Prentice Hall Press, 1986

Rowley, Nancy J. "Red Cross Quilts for the Great War", in *Uncoverings*, vol. 3, 1982

Safford, Carleton L., & Robert Bishop. *America's Quilts and Coverlets.* New York: E.P. Dutton & Co. Inc., 1972

Sater, Joel. *The Patchwork Quilt.* Ephrata, Pennsylvania: Science Press, 1981

Smith, Wilene. "Quilt Blocks—or—Quilt *Patterns*.", in *Uncoverings*, vol. 7, 1986

Swan, Susan Burrows. *A Winterthur Guide to American Needlework.* New York: Crown Publishers Inc., 1976, with The Henry Francis DuPont Winterthur Museum

Swan, Susan Burrows. *Plain & Fancy: American Women and Their Needlework, 1700-1850.* New York: Holt, Rinehart & Winston, 1977

Uncoverings. A series of research papers of The American Quilt Study Group. Mill Valley, California: American Quilt Study Group, 1980-1993. Edited by Sally Garoutte, 1980-1987; Laurel Horton, 1988-1993

Waldvogel, Merikay. *Soft Covers for Hard Times: Quiltmaking & the Great Depression.* Nashville, Tennessee: Rutledge Hill Press, 1990

Webster, Marie D. *Quilts: Their Story and How to Make Them.* Garden City, New York: Doubleday, Page & Co., 1915, reprinted by Gale Research Company, Detroit, 1972

Weissman, Judith Reiter, & Wendy Lavitt. *Labors of Love: America's Textiles and Needlework, 1650-1930.* New York: Alfred A. Knopf, 1987

Woodard, Thos. K., & Blanche Greenstein. *Twentieth Century Quilts, 1900-1950.* New York: E.P. Dutton, 1988

Care and conservation

Bogle, Michael. *Textile Conservation Centre Notes*—#9 "Packing and Shipping Data for Textiles"; #12 "Museum Lighting for Textiles"; #13 "Museum Display of Textiles"; #14 "The Storage of Textiles"; #15 "The Mounting of Textiles for Storage and Display". North Andover, Massachusetts: Merrimack Valley Textile Museum, 1979

Canadian Conservation Institute. *Notes*—#13/1 "Textiles and the Environment", 1992; #13/2 "Flat Storage for Textiles", 1993; #13/3 "Rolled Storage for Textiles", 1993; #13/4 "Velcro Support System for Textiles", 1990; #13/6 "Mounting Small, Light, Flat Textiles", 1995; #13/7 "Washing Non-Coloured Textiles", 1993; #13/8 "Applying Accession Numbers to Textiles", 1992; #13/9 "Anionic Detergent", 1992; #13/10 "Stitches Used in Textiles Conservation", 1995. Ottawa, Ontario: Canadian Conservation Institute

Cognac, Camille Dalphond. *Quilt Restoration: A Practical Guide.* McLean, Virginia: EPM Publications, 1994

Gunn, Virginia. "The Care and Conservation of Quilts", in *Technical Guide #3.* San Francisco: American Quilt Study Group, 1988

Gunn, Virginia. "The Display, Care, and Conservation of Old Quilts", in *In the Heart of Pennsylvania: Symposium Papers.* Lewisburg, Pennsylvania: Oral Traditions Project of the Union County Historical Society, 1986; p. 90-95

Gunn, Virginia. "New Thoughts on Care and Conservation", in *Pieced by Mother: Symposium Papers.* Lewisburg, Pennsylvania: Oral Traditions Project of the Union County Historical Society, 1988; p. 115-119

Kile, Michael. "The Collector: Free Spirit in the West", in *The Quilt Digest*, no. 1. San Francisco, California: Kiracofe & Kile, 1983, p. 56-61 [article about the mounting of the Esprit collection]

Leene, Jentina E., ed. *Textile Conservation.* England: The Butterworth Group, 1972, & the International Institute for Conservation of Historic and Artistic Works; also Washington, D.C.: Smithsonian Institution Press, [1974?]

Orlofsky, Patsy. "The Collector's Guide for the Care of Quilts in the Home", in *The Quilt Digest*, no. 2, 1984, p. 58-69. San Francisco, California: Kiracofe & Kile

Puentes, Nancy O'Bryant. *First Aid for Family Quilts.* Wheatridge, Colorado: Moon Over the Mountain Publishing, 1986